THE FINANCIAL COACHING *Playbook*

BY KELSA DICKEY

ISBN: 978-0-5786023-2-5 (Paperback)
Library of Congress Control Number: 2019953940

All content reflects our opinion at a given time and can change as time progresses. All information should be taken as an opinion and should not be misconstrued for professional or legal advice. The contents of this book are informational in nature and are not legal or tax advice, and the authors and publishers are not engaged in the provision of legal, tax, or any other advice.

Front cover image and Book Design by Kelly Teno, Trüce Creative | www.trücecreative.com
Printed by Financial Coach Academy in the United States of America.
First printing edition 2020.

Financial Coach Academy
333 E Cullumber Ave
Gilbert, AZ 85234
www.financialcoachacademy.com

TO MY HUSBAND, MICHAEL.

THIS AMAZING JOURNEY OF FINANCIAL COACHING

IS ALL BECAUSE YOU BELIEVED IN ME.

WE ARE THE BEST KIND OF TEAM.

I love you.

THE
FINANCIAL
COACHING
Playbook

By Kelsa Dickey

Table of Contents

I knew I loved to coach but only saw it as helping people with their budgets. Financial Coach Academy helped me realize there is so much more involved than just numbers. I love financial coaching because I get to help people get clarity on their financial situation and show them how they can live the life they want while managing their finances with confidence. It's extremely rewarding to see the transformation that happens not just with their money habits, but in their family, relationships, and day-to-day lives. You can't put a price on that kind of transformation.

CYNDIA RIVERA

FAMILY FINANCES REDESIGNED

Chapter 01

Getting Started As A Financial Coach

Mind The Gap

As I was compiling the information for this book, a survey was released by The Associated Press-NORC Center for Public Affairs Research. It said roughly two-thirds of Americans (67%) describe their overall financial situation as "generally good."

However, the same survey revealed the deep anxiety and vulnerability that underlies this outward optimism. Nearly 4 in 10 people said they aren't sure they could cover an emergency expense of $1,000. Only 2 in 10 described themselves as "very confident" that they will have enough money in savings for retirement. Almost half said they had "little or no confidence" they'll be able to save enough.

| UNCERTAINTY OF EMERGENCY FUNDS | UNCERTAINTY OF ENOUGH SAVINGS | UNCERTAINTY OF RETIREMENT |

About 3 in 4 people nearing retirement age said they feel pretty good about their financial circumstances, although almost one-third of those over age 50 said they are unprepared for retirement, and about 2 in 10 think they won't be able to stop working. Of people surveyed under age 30, 4 in 10 called their current financial situations "poor," and 56% said they don't feel they'll be prepared for retirement.

As a financial coach, that confusing gap – between brave optimism and sheer panic – is the area I specialize in. I help people see and confront the core beliefs and spending habits that might be holding them back. I help them home-in on their goals and dreams and make progress toward meeting them.

Most folks are resilient. They figure if they work hard, things will work out, even if they have to juggle expenses or pull out a credit card from time to time. But too often, they end up feeling like they're riding a monthly roller coaster, hoping they're strapped in well enough to survive.

There's a better way to live. Wouldn't you like to show people how to get there?

What The Heck Is A Financial Coach?

A decade ago, the idea of being a financial coach was totally foreign to me. I used to quip that it was a title I simply made up. Michael, my husband and business partner, would gush, *"You're the best financial coach I know!"* It became our running joke – because, of course, I was the only one he knew.

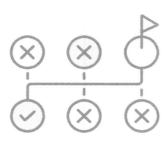 Today, I love being a financial coach – love it to my core! I can't tell you how rewarding it is to help people bring their own financial strengths and pitfalls into focus and learn how to manage them. And my goal in this book is to share the ideas, strategies, and lessons gleaned from my own ups and downs in this business so that you can help people in similar ways and learn to love it, too.

Financial coaching isn't quite like any other business I know. It doesn't purely emphasize numbers and sales, like financial advising. It doesn't emphasize mindset and emotions, like life coaching and most forms of business coaching. It is a precise balance of both – and because of this, your business model needs to be completely different than those other industries. You need to show your experience and financial journey so your clients get to know, like, and trust you. You need to have some conceptual knowledge of finances, but you also need to have coaching skills. Together, they are a useful and even fun blend of traits that can serve your clients well and make for a rewarding career path.

What began at my dining room table as a hobby is now a business that brings in a quarter-million dollars each year. In 2016 our beautiful daughter Carmen Jillian – "CJ" for short – came along, and I slammed into the reality of juggling parenthood with my booming and rewarding financial coaching business. Our son Alex joined the family in 2019.

...look at problems as opportunities.

It might sound a little naive, but when I realized I couldn't be everywhere or help everyone, it was honestly a sad moment. However, as an entrepreneur for the past 10 years, one thing I've learned is to look at problems as opportunities. If I don't like the answer, the next question is, *"So, what am I going to do about it?"*

In this case, the answer was to create the Financial Coach Academy. No, I might not be able to help everyone. But I can train wonderful people like you, who have the same desire to help others, and prepare YOU to step into the role of financial coach, confidently and proudly. Together, maybe we can help everyone!

How To Use This Book

Most people go into business for themselves feeling hopeful and highly motivated. They're thrilled at the prospect of making their own decisions and setting their own priorities. They'll be the masters of their own schedules – imagine the flexibility!

In most cases, the reality is a lot more challenging. Entrepreneurship can be a bumpy road and this playbook is meant to help you avoid some of the potholes. You may find yourself in a rut one month and excited the next. Feeling self-doubt one week, then brimming with ideas the next. You may find yourself putting off certain steps in the process of opening your doors – convincing yourself that everything has to be perfect – when really, it does not.

I've packed as much information as I can into this playbook – shortcuts, lessons and some best practices – but it's only the framework. Along the way, you'll need to tap into your own creativity and use your intuition to develop your coaching business and make it work for you.

In the next eight chapters, we will cover:

How to determine what kind of coaching business you want to create.

How to decide the types of clients you want to work with.

The basics of setting up shop as a financial coach.

Tips for designing every step of your coaching program: from first contact, to the goals and skills you want clients to take away from this experience.

How to have sales conversations with prospective clients and respond to the questions, concerns, and/or objections you might encounter.

Strategies for creating interesting, meaningful content about financial topics to share with clients, along with online resources for assistance.

How to help clients set goals and examine their values and fears around money.

Teach clients how to use the Ultimate Financial Power Plan: a method I've created for budgeting and paying off debt.

Ways to market your coaching services effectively, including developing and working with referral partners.

Additional services you can use to grow your business, from daily money management to financial wellness workshops for businesses.

Some of the playbook content is designed for self-reflection, helping you home-in on the kinds of financial issues and clientele you want to work with. You'll want to use those worksheets as you read the chapters in which they are mentioned. Other content is for sharing, or adapting to share, with clients.

The goal is to provide you with clarity of purpose and a streamlined, successful system for running your business. I truly believe the more efficient, organized, and effective you are in conducting your business, the more focus and attention you'll be able to provide your clients. They'll feel better supported, they'll get better results, and they'll be lifelong, loyal clients for you. Your business will be that much more successful because of the strong foundation we build together, using this book.

Yes, it's a lot to cover! And you might not do it all flawlessly, especially when you first start out.

In my experience, most financial coaches have perfectionist tendencies. This comes from a desire to not be criticized, or not receive feedback, or not be embarrassed – thinking, 'If I'm perfect, I'll avoid all of that.' Perfection may be a protective shield. But on the flip side, perfection is also the enemy of greatness. You can't grow and improve if you won't listen to and learn from feedback.

...perfection is also the enemy of greatness.

So, accept the fact that, with your first few clients, you might be nervous or even scared. That does not mean you won't know how to help them!

It's easy to compare your prospective clients' financial lives to being on a roller coaster. And for you, self-employment can be a roller coaster too. The advice you'll get here won't prevent your belly from dropping, but it shouldn't keep you from getting on the ride at all. Think of it instead as the guidance of a seasoned rider, reminding you to buckle up, hang on tight, scream as loud as you want, and laugh as often as possible through the twists, turns, and loops!

It's important to note that my purpose is not to create a bunch of mini-Kelsas. You don't have to adopt my financial philosophy, my beliefs, or even my coaching style. In these pages, you might even read some ideas or philosophies about spending, saving, and budgeting that you don't agree with. Remember this: personal finance is personal! The key is not to follow the book in literal terms, but to use the lessons as inspiration and guideposts for turning your own financial principles and practices into skills and exercises for others to follow.

we're in the "transformational" business.

I do hope you feel inspired by what you learn in these pages. However, as financial coaches, we are not in the "inspirational" business – we're in the "transformational" business. Our goal for our clients is that they take action, dig in, and do something with the inspiration they feel, working with us.

Thank you for allowing me to be a part of your journey as a financial coach and for being part of mine. Thank you for being part of mine. Thank you for helping me to fulfill my mission of taking the stress out of money for so many people who desperately need a new and caring approach to their personal finances.

Let's Get Started

This is a day to be celebrated. By picking up this book, it's the first day that you've decided to create something spectacular. You're going to put in a lot of work and effort. You're going to really push yourself. You're putting in your time and energy, and investing in yourself – all this is definitely worth celebrating!

Whenever I start to work with a new client, I feel much the same kind of excitement. I see it as the first day of the rest of their lives – and I know that I'll be able to help them to make their lives better. However, it's also during the first meeting that I typically remind the client to be patient and trust the process. We're making long-term changes here, not doing sprints, and it's important to manage emotions and expectations.

The same holds true for those who participate in my Financial Coach Academy. It's great that we're excited to be making changes. But managing your own expectations is part of the process as you gain clarity and create an overview of your new business.

With that said, I'm also going to ask that you make a commitment to dive in – fully, completely, and with your fear right alongside you. I won't ask you to jump in without fear, just despite it. I'm willing to bet most people who have a desire to be a financial coach have similar personalities – we're probably 'Type A' planners, organized, proactive, intentional – as I've already mentioned, we are likely total perfectionists. We plan at least three steps out – and that's good, especially for the clients. It's a skill that will serve you well as a financial coach.

And yet, when it comes to being a business owner, I think this is the single trait we all need to squash. Here's why: You cannot wait to have everything figured out before you move forward. So, as a small business owner, I believe in the theory of MESSY ACTION! When you take a leap of faith as a perfectionist, you must understand that the first time you do ANYTHING won't likely be the way you'll continue to do it. You'll want to make it even better, of course!

The important point here is to not over-think things. Jump in! Rather than simply consuming the information and mulling it over endlessly, be decisive, implement, and be an active learner who creates.

As we hit the ground running, your to-do list of tasks and assignments may seem overwhelming at times. Remember, you're creating a new business! My goal is that, by the time you finish this playbook, you absolutely feel ready to meet with clients. On your end, it's important to schedule time on your calendar every day to devote to this process.

> "Have a bias towards action – let's see something happen now. You can break that big plan into small steps and take the first step right away."
>
> - INDIRA GANDHI, POLITICIAN AND STATESWOMAN

Broaden Your Perspective

Oftentimes, people who become financial coaches start because of the impact they believe they can have on others. They see people struggling with a particular problem – money – and they want to try to help them solve it. At the same time, the new coach may have a very limited view of the positive impact this line of work can have on his or her own life. My clients have attended my baby showers; I've attended their weddings, graduation parties, and holiday parties. We get together for pool parties and football games.

Recently, my assistant Sheri's oldest son was diagnosed with Stage 4 cancer, which rocked our small, close-knit business to its core, as you might imagine. With Sheri's permission, I sent out an email letting everyone know. Within an hour, a financial advisor who sends us business came to our office – just to give hugs and show support. Other clients sent gifts, cards, money, and meals for Sheri's family. We all shed a few tears.

My point is that it's been incredible to see the village that we've created and how truly supportive it is, from all perspectives.

You may be wondering, "What does this have to do with being a successful coach?"

Everything, I think.

Yes, I make what I consider "good money," and I'm incredibly proud of and grateful for that. What is more important to me is that I do it by building strong relationships with people I want to help, and who want to be helped. The result happens to be that I'm able to support my family by doing this.

You surely have your own valid and heartfelt reasons for wanting to be a financial coach. They most likely include this vision of being happier or enjoying what you're doing more than you do now. I'm here to say that, as bright a picture as you're imagining, it isn't even close to how good it can really be! Not only will you have a big impact on your clients, it's likely your clients will have a big impact on you, as well. So THAT should be part of your motivation for moving through this playbook with gusto.

I don't mean to be morbid here, but if I were to die, I KNOW my funeral would be full of my clients who are there to say goodbye, and I KNOW they would say beautiful things about me. I'm surrounded every day by people I truly enjoy. They became friends, a really big part of my life in all sorts of ways. I get cards, emails, texts – every single month – thanking me for saving a marriage or changing a life. In how many professions can you say that happens?

As I see and feel gratitude for what I do, it makes me feel amazing for the impact I can have on this world in my own, small way. I SEE the impact I have. I get to EXPERIENCE that impact.

Michael has dubbed this "Kelsa's Trifecta." The idea is that I get to help people every day and in turn, their results, dedication, and commitment empower me. And we make good money. That's the sweet spot. That's also the kind of business we're going to show you how to create.

We're shooting for the TRIFECTA.

KELSA'S TRIFECTA

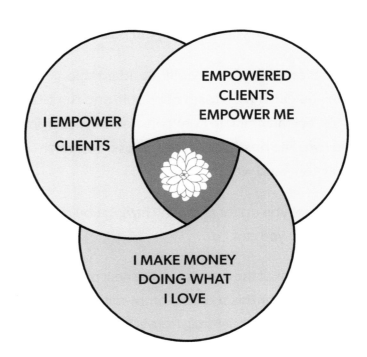

I EMPOWER CLIENTS

EMPOWERED CLIENTS EMPOWER ME

I MAKE MONEY DOING WHAT I LOVE

WE'VE FAILED IF...

 You make money helping your clients, but they're people you don't really enjoy or they're sucking the energy out of you.

 You help people and you love them, and they lift you up – but you're going broke in the process.

 You make money trying to help people you like, but you're not getting them results.

Visualize Your Business Success

While I'm sure you are anxious to learn how to set your prices, design your programs, and start marketing your services to clients, we have to start digging a little more slowly in order to build a solid foundation for your business.

One of the first aspects of financial coaching that must be clarified is the role you want your financial coaching business to play in your life. *What does success look like to you? What is the vision you have for your business?*

Financial coaching is a beautifully adaptable skill. You can do it from home once in a while, you can have a team of people and run a business that is helping hundreds of people, and anything in between. You can coach in person or online, or a combination of the two. The possibilities are endless. So, which of these options do you have in mind for yourself – and why?

Let's not set you up for failure by having you design something you don't fully believe in or believe you can't do.

It's time to look at the exercise on the next page entitled *What Kind of Business Do I Want?* Working through this should prompt some serious thought about how you envision your financial coaching business, from whether you want an office to whether you're willing to travel for business, to how much you want to do yourself versus contract out to others.

Let's begin by helping you gain clarity on who you are as a coach, why you want to help, who your ideal client is, and what financial situations you will help those clients with.

If you commit to completing these initial few steps, the steps that follow become easier. On the other hand, if you skip these steps, everything else will feel forced or uninspired.

When you imagine yourself sitting across the table from your client(s), what do you think they'll want to hear from you? And more important, what kinds of expertise do you feel strongly about being able to provide to them?

What Kind of Business Do I Want?

HOME BASED	☐ ☐ ☐ ☐ ☐ ☐ ☐ ☐ ☐	OFFICE
VIRTUAL	☐ ☐ ☐ ☐ ☐ ☐ ☐ ☐ ☐	FACE-TO-FACE
PART TIME	☐ ☐ ☐ ☐ ☐ ☐ ☐ ☐ ☐	FULL TIME
EMPLOYEES	☐ ☐ ☐ ☐ ☐ ☐ ☐ ☐ ☐	OUTSOURCED
TRAVEL	☐ ☐ ☐ ☐ ☐ ☐ ☐ ☐ ☐	STAY AT HOME
GENERALIST	☐ ☐ ☐ ☐ ☐ ☐ ☐ ☐ ☐	EXPERT
MASS MARKET $	☐ ☐ ☐ ☐ ☐ ☐ ☐ ☐ ☐	HIGH END $$$
LARGE COMMUNITY	☐ ☐ ☐ ☐ ☐ ☐ ☐ ☐ ☐	PRIVATE CONVERSATIONS
COMMITMENT	☐ ☐ ☐ ☐ ☐ ☐ ☐ ☐ ☐	MONTH TO MONTH
NATIONAL	☐ ☐ ☐ ☐ ☐ ☐ ☐ ☐ ☐	LOCAL
DONE-FOR-YOU	☐ ☐ ☐ ☐ ☐ ☐ ☐ ☐ ☐	DO-IT-YOURSELF
MAKE MONEY	☐ ☐ ☐ ☐ ☐ ☐ ☐ ☐ ☐	MAKE A DIFFERENCE

NOTES

There are so many aspects of personal finance to consider, and you'll naturally be drawn to some more than others. Give this some serious thought.

Can you see yourself relating to young parents who are juggling student loan debt with everyday expenses and helping them to master budgeting basics?

Do you want to work with people with bad credit to improve it and "step back from the brink?"

Or would you be more interested in helping single women in their 50s and 60s whose life circumstances have left them wondering how to manage the day-to-day finances after the loss of a loved one?

Or are you more comfortable with folks who have a big wish list and a decent income, but haven't been able to set aside the money to fund any of the items on that list, and can't figure out why?

Those are just a few examples, but the point here is that you will be most effective when you're providing the kinds of advice that you are most adept at giving.

You might think, *"Well, I want to help all of them!"* But as you'll read in the next section of this chapter, Find Your Ideal Client, there are better reasons to narrow it down. At the Financial Coach Academy, we've developed a method for coaches to determine the top problems they feel confident in their ability to solve and that their ideal clients can identify with the most.

Start by brainstorming 10 topics you could teach as workshops, you feel called to address, and you think your target clients would want to learn. Even if you don't have a desire to hold workshops as part of your business strategy, thinking about the topics being taught in a workshop setting makes them more tangible. Then rank these topics to discover which ones are what we call "SUP2ER Problems."

SUP2ER Problems

 ### PECIFIC

How succinctly can this problem be stated? Exactly what is it?

 ### RGENT

How quickly do they need this problem solved before something bad happens?

 ### ERVASIVE

Is this a problem any person would have in their financial life, or is it only an issue with this client?

 ### ERSISTENT

How often does this problem come up for the client? Does it keep coming back?

 ### XPENSIVE

How much is their problem costing them?
(*High interest on debt, penalties for back taxes, etc.*)

 ### ECOGNIZABLE

Does the client truly understand the importance of solving this problem?

When thinking about your ideal client, how important is this problem to *them*?

Rank each topic below from 1 to 10:
(10 meaning MOST important to that client; 1 meaning LEAST important), based on the SUP2ER factors from page 13:

Ten Topics I Could Teach As Workshops...

Topic Idea	Ranking 1 - 10

When you total the rankings for each workshop idea, a pattern emerges, guiding you naturally to the topics or problems that will be most beneficial for you to focus on in your marketing efforts.

Once you can clearly identify the problems you want to help people solve, it's a lot easier to determine exactly who experiences those problems. This person is your ideal client, and you'll want to be able to describe them in detail.

Find Your Ideal Client

Your ideal client is EVERYTHING. In almost any industry, when people first start a business, their tendency is to cast a wide net to attract thousands of people. They're going for quantity! They want any client that will allow them to help.

But if your net is cast too widely, you end up not attracting anyone – simply because you're not talking or resonating with any individual person.

Once you identify your niche, marketing becomes much simpler because you know who you're talking to. You can design a program that addresses their exact problem because you can identify that problem almost effortlessly.

Yes, we may all be financial coaches who help people with money, but some will decide they want to help folks who are nearing retirement. Others will focus on young adults, or those going through a divorce, people with debt, people in major life transitions, and so on.

If you try to help the wrong person – and by that, I mean "wrong" for your personality, or your skill set, or your money philosophy – they won't move forward or get the results you're both hoping to see. And this will undermine your own confidence, perhaps even derail your ultimate chances for coaching success.

Working with the wrong client can make you question everything: Am I really cut out for this? Was this a bad idea? Why am I not getting results for this client? The solution?

Find your favorite client.

I wish I would have done this early on, which is why I'm asking you to take this all-important step early in this process. When I began coaching, I started by helping anyone and everyone, and some of these relationships were difficult.

In building my own business, as well as helping others become financial coaches through the Academy, I have come to learn you don't "pick" a niche or client type as much as you are guided to them – if you allow yourself to be. How does this happen?

With every client experience and interaction, pay close attention to:

- What you enjoyed? What flowed?

- What felt clunky?

- Where did your skills gap?

- Who makes you feel like working even harder for them?

- Who makes you smile, laugh, and feel good about yourself?

- Who joyfully paid your fees?

- Who constantly tries to renegotiate or bargain, like your efforts are some kind of digital garage sale?

It's likely that with every conversation, your dream client will come more clearly into focus. As my lens became clearer, I adjusted my marketing to speak directly to that person.

The truth is, I've experienced everything my dream client has. I deeply relate to this person. So, don't try really hard to define your customer avatar; simply reflect on your experiences and see that person form.

This insight freed me to be myself in every aspect of my business. I don't have to self-edit or "pose" to fit in. If I did, my dream client wouldn't recognize me. I discovered this by allowing myself to be organically guided to my niche instead of assigning the task of figuring it out to my over-thinking mind.

Niche clarity isn't about deciding what you want to do and who you think needs it. For some, it can be an organic unfolding that happens over time as you tune into the world around you. Some would say, you don't decide your niche. You are guided to it by paying attention to experiences with curious fascination.

The key to niche clarity is to reflect and inquire. Take action in order to gain awareness and insights.

1. What work do you want to bring into the world? Describe it.

2. Who do you envision serving with this work?

3. Have you met someone that fits this vision? Perhaps a friend, a past client, a relative? What qualities makes this person a good fit for you?

4. Using their words, what symptoms and discomforts does this person struggle with?

5. What does this person want instead?

6. Before working with you, what did this individual do to try to eliminate her/his symptoms?

7. Why didn't she/he succeed?

8. What about your solution will feel like a miracle to that person?

9. What results can she/he look forward to?

10. What results have you helped someone create?

Let's pull it all together. Use the template (below) to create your Dream Client Profile Paragraph.

My dream client is someone who is (select some qualities from question #2). She/he is seeking a resource to help her/him create (select something from question #5). Not creating this is painful because it means she/he must live with (something from question #4). She/he has tried (something from question #6). But, frustratingly, that didn't work due to (something from #7). Because I (something from #1) that is (something from #8), she/he can enjoy (something from #9).

Create Your "Why Story"

Mark Twain said it perfectly: *"The two most important days in your life are the day you are born, and the day you find out why."*

The next assignment is creating your "Why Story" – describing the reasons you want to be a financial coach. These are the reasons that drive you forward and give your efforts purpose.

This assignment isn't only about figuring out your "why." It's about crafting a compelling story that people will want to hear, a story you can share with an individual or a group, with such passion and in just enough detail that it works for that audience.

It's about digging deep and being vulnerable, so your clients will trust that they can be vulnerable with you, too. And it's about understanding how this purpose-driven story connects to an ideal individual whom you can help.

I'm going to start by telling you my story. Read it as if you're a potential client looking for help, seeking someone who can eliminate your financial stress. There's a big reason I'm sharing this story with you – and it isn't just so you know more about me.

My "Why Story"

I know exactly when I decided to help people with their money. One afternoon, when I was middle-school age, I remember sitting on the couch at home watching TV, while my sisters, both cheerleaders, were practicing their routines in the family room.

I noticed my Mom sitting at the dining room table, seemingly oblivious to the racket coming from the TV and my cheering siblings. In front of her: a stack of papers and another pile of unopened mail, a calculator, a pad of paper, and pens. She hung her head, and I heard her sigh deeply. She sat there for a long time.

Mom was a social worker for the State of Michigan. It was a good job, and she was good at it – she worked hard and cared passionately for the people she tried to help. But when the paychecks and the bills rolled in, she sat for hours trying to juggle them and manage the money, and never could seem to wrestle control of our family finances.

A few weeks later, there was a knock at our door and my aunt walked in. They embraced, and I saw that Mom was crying. *"I had to file for bankruptcy,"* she sobbed.

My aunt held her and said, over and over again, *"It's gonna be okay."* As a young kid, I didn't know what bankruptcy was, just that it had to do with money and it was bad. But I learned that day that money has an impact on your life – sometimes good, sometimes bad. It's the game we're all forced to play.

When I was a high school senior, a college recruiter came to our school and asked, *"What do you want to do with your life?"* I said, *"I want to help people with their money."* He said, *"Great! You should become a financial advisor!"*

So, I got a degree in finance, became fully licensed as a financial advisor, and practiced for three years. I hated every minute of it. The position was commission-based, so I had the incentive to sell the client the product with the biggest commission, not necessarily what I thought was best for them. I realized the clients I enjoyed helping were the ones who wanted help getting out of debt or learning how to budget. I didn't enjoy the investment side of things, the "wealth management" aspects of the job.

I called it my "quarter-life crisis." I was still very young and had gone into financial advising thinking it'd be a dream come true! I'd be so happy working at my passion every day, helping people with their money!

At that point, I told myself, *"A job is just a job – I don't have to love it. I just have to be good at it and it has to pay the bills."* I went back to school, got a Master's degree, and entered the corporate accounting field, where I spent the next six years. I was good at it and enjoyed some aspects of it. But whenever I could, I was still helping people with their money.

I remember walking into a coworker's cubicle one day. Visibly upset, Rosemary explained she'd just gotten into a fight with her spouse over money that morning, *"We got this bill, we don't know how to pay it."* I told her the same thing I'd been saying to people for years: *"Why don't you come over after work and I'll take a look at it? Let me see what I can do."*

I did this for a number of people, after work or on weekends – and one day, I was driving home from work exhausted and cranky, and knowing I'd go back to the office in the morning and find another mountain of work and another 12-hour day ahead of me. And that evening, as tired as I was, I still had to meet with a client.

But here's the revelation – after an hour, the client would leave and I realized I felt invigorated and energized working with that person. The one hour I spent as a financial coach was the best hour of my entire day. I had to do more of it!

I told my husband, *"I don't know how this is going to happen, but this is what I was meant to do, and I have to give it a try. I have to try being a financial coach full-time – and if I don't succeed, it's okay, I can always go back to corporate America."*

We spent about a year planning, and that is when Fiscal Fitness Phoenix was born. I left the corporate world on March 25, 2011 – and since then, I have loved every minute of helping people take the stress out of money.

Now, think about the people I described in my "Why Story."

Who did I describe?

- ✓ Someone who wasn't present in the moment because of financial stress
- ✓ Someone who tried really hard and still couldn't get things under control
- ✓ Someone who worked hard and had a good job
- ✓ Someone who was affected emotionally by the worry over money

In the story, I also described myself as:

- ✓ Someone who has experienced a career crisis
- ✓ Someone who wasn't happy, and had to do something about it
- ✓ Someone who made assumptions about life and then shifted their perspective
- ✓ Someone who is educated

In other words, by telling this story I give the person who's hearing it some insight into who I am, while at the same time connecting with my ideal client.

Creating your own *"Why Story"* isn't just a matter of writing down the facts, dates, and events that shaped your decision to enter this field. It is a matter of taking those facts, dates, and events and crafting them into a compelling story. Your purpose may not stem from a childhood memory like mine. Your "Why Story" could start later in life.

By "crafting," I certainly don't mean making stuff up! I mean: give careful thought to what to include or leave out, when to describe something in detail and when to leave out the particulars.

It can be helpful to start with an outline, then fill in the details. And think of it like an accordion – you'll be able to expand or condense the story details as needed, depending on your audience, but the main points are always there.

Let's acknowledge here that this process requires honest introspection, which can be tougher than it sounds. Your story is innately related to who you are as a person, and in some cases, it can be a hard story to tell. You might have to admit that you did something dumb or made mistakes.

In my case, I had to admit my Mom was broke, and we grew up broke. When I chose to share that story, not everyone in my family was happy about it – money is often considered a taboo topic in families, and the lack of it even more so.

In these situations, focus on the growth you achieved, or other positive takeaways as a result. Focus on the good outcome and the motivating factors. You've got to dig deep, because what will resonate with the people you want to help is that you have authentic life experiences – good and bad – that led you to this place, this calling, this desire to help others.

... money is often a taboo topic in families

Do not try to use anyone else's WHY! It's tempting to co-opt a great story. But you have yours already – you just have to discover it or tell it in a compelling way. And once you have it, you'll be able to call on it for the rest of your career as a financial coach!

Knowing your "why" early in this training is what will help you create your business message, discover your perfect client with clarity, and explain why you do what you do. It's the spirit of your business and a key to creating a relationship with your clients.

It is also your own statement of purpose that can keep you moving forward on the tough days – because sometimes, yes, there will be tough days.

Your "Why Story"

Gather your thoughts below to start on your own "Why Story!"

What are the financial challenges you have overcome in your life?

What was the impact of those financial challenges?
Physically, emotionally, spiritually, mentally, financially?

What new results or possibilities opened up as a result of overcoming them?

What 3 qualities have you gained from this journey?

What makes you come alive, brings you joy, fulfillment, and excitement?

What are your innate strengths?

What do those close to you think your innate strengths are?

Where do you add the greatest value?

How will you measure your life?

What is your purpose in life?

What is your why?

What words would you use to describe your purpose?

On the next page, you will find the exercise '7 Signature Stories', by Karen Dietz, author of *Storytelling for Dummies*. This is a handy summary of some general topics that make for compelling stories. You'll find these useful not only in crafting your own "Why Story," but in creating presentations and planning your marketing.

7 Signature Stories

YOUR SIGNATURE STORIES	PURPOSE
1. Origin Story – the story of how you got started. Your "why" story, and what makes you different from your competitors.	To convey what makes you different and unique; to set you apart from the competition, to build trust.
2. People & Results Stories (PR) – stories about customers, vendors, employees, stakeholders. How customers were able to do something extraordinary because you helped them. How vendors, employees, stakeholders did something extraordinary.	To convey the results you produce. The amazing things your staff and vendors do. Replaces the case study. Used in sales as 3rd party stories to make the sale. Builds pride and sales.
3. Values In Action Stories – stories about how you or people in your company live your values.	To convey that you walk your talk, that your actions match what you say. Conveys what is most important to you, and what is unique about you/your business. Builds trust and inspires.
4. Product/Service Stories – the back stories about how your products or services came to be created and why. Different from your Origin Story.	To satisfy people's curiosity; to share why a product/service was created, challenges faced and overcome; another way to build trust, pride; also inspires.
5. Why I... Story – the story about what keeps you going when times get tough. What keeps you motivated. What gets you out of bed in the morning.	To convey dependability and trustworthiness. People want to know you'll be there for them when the going gets tough.
6. Lessons Learned Stories – stories about mistakes or failures you've had, and what you've learned; what you do differently today; what decisions you made because of that experience.	To convey wisdom, humbleness, authenticity. Use this story only at the right time with the right audience. Builds trust and personal presence.
7. Future Story – the story about what you and your customers together are doing today to make a better tomorrow.	To convey the difference you make in the world, the impact you have, what future vision you are living into.
Which ones are your favorite to share?	**Choose 1 - 3 of your favorites.**

Coach Or Consultant?

A final thought to consider – how do you want to be known? What do you want to call yourself when someone asks, *"What do you do?"*

As you take the steps outlined in Chapter 2 to get your business started, it will be time to pick a job title – the term you'll use to identify yourself to the public. Yes, this is the Financial Coaching Playbook, but many people see a substantial difference between a coach, a consultant, a trainer, etc.

Have you ever heard this kind of complaint? *"I spent $15K on a Business Coach, but I feel like she didn't really teach me anything. I really just wanted someone to TELL me what to do for my business!"*

There's no right or wrong title. It's just important to gain clarity as you move forward to create your business identity, and the descriptions, programs, and prices you will use in your role with clients.

So, please ponder this topic and decide how you see yourself and how you plan to present yourself to the world.

> "People don't just buy WHAT you do,
> they buy WHY you do it."
>
> - SIMON SINEK, AUTHOR

Chapter 01

Action Summary

☐ **1. Clarify your vision & define business success:**

    a. Determine the vision for the impact your business will have on your life.

    b. Define what business success looks like to you.

☐ **2. Identify your ideal client:**

    a. Determine the chief problems you want to help clients resolve.

    b. Understand the characteristics of your ideal client.

    c. Write out your Dream Client Profile.

☐ **3. Craft your "Why Story:"**

    a. Identify the details and pivotal experiences that determine your Why by answering the questions provided.

    b. Craft the details above into a compelling story .

    c. Practice your "Why Story" often.

☐ **4. Begin outlining the 7 Signature Stories you may use in your business.**

☐ **5. Choose the title that resonates best with you - Coach, Trainer, Consultant, etc.**

The **two** **MOST** **IMPORTANT** OF days YOUR life ARE THE DAY YOU WERE **BORN** & THE DAY YOU find out **WHY**

• MARK TWAIN •

Creating my Q & A session was very much THE "aha" moment for me… the aha moment came when I realized not all prospective clients are ready to work with me, or are coach-able. You just need to be prepared to align them with another option, be that another coach, advisor, counselor, etc.

JOLANTA GONET-THOMAS

IRONWOOD FINANCIAL COACHING

"

Chapter 02

Setting Up Shop & Inviting Your Ideal Client To Work With You

Now that we've covered who you are as a coach and why you want to do this, it's time to set up your business to attract the types of clients you want to help. When someone calls or reaches out to you, it's important to know what to say and how to get them scheduled. But first, you'll need to get all set up and ready to accept clients! This is neither difficult nor expensive, although it takes some time and care to get it right. Some of these initial steps aren't sexy or glamorous, but they're important nonetheless.

First Impressions

Working for yourself has built-in challenges. The first you'll encounter is convincing people that this is a real business, and you're on the job even if you work from home! There are tips from many sources about making a good first impression as a self-employed person. Here are the preliminary steps that, in my experience, are necessary for financial coaching:

Set up your business phone.

Set up a separate, Google voice phone number that you can answer professionally: *"Hi, this is Coach Kelsa with Fiscal Fitness. How can I help you?"*

Script out the content of your message – make it short, upbeat, and say you'll return the call promptly. Your three-year-old's voicemail greeting on the home phone may indeed be adorable, but that's not the way to attract clients who need financial coaching. If you decide to have music playing in the background, choose this wisely. Some people ask why they can't just use their cell phone as their business line. In my experience, this is asking for trouble. Inevitably, you'll encounter clients who feel they can call (or text) anytime to ask anything. Share your cell number and you'll live to regret it.

Set up a separate, business email address.

The easiest option here is a Gmail account, although Google also allows people to set up a professional email address for as little as $6 per month through its G Suite service. (Look online at gsuite.google.com/pricing.html for details and pricing information).

Customize your email signature line. This might include a clean, simple logo if you've created one, or a photo of yourself, along with all your contact info: phone, email, website, mailing address. WiseStamp (wisestamp.com) allows you to create a custom signature line free of charge, but may trigger a spam response to your emails. You can also search "Gmail signature tutorial" in YouTube for instructional videos to walk you through the process.

Rent a private mailbox (PMB) or Post Office box.

This isn't a requirement, but it's definitely an option for people who live alone or simply don't want to use their home address for non-email business correspondence or on a website. If you have a strong relationship with another professional, such as a CPA or financial advisor for example, you can also ask to use their address.

Print your business cards.

There are several easy-to-use websites that offer attractive business cards at low prices. Vista Print (vistaprint.com) and Moo (moo.com/us) are two that come to mind. You can also visit your local Staples. You can upload your logo and design your own cards, or choose from hundreds of templates. If you're going to have a website, be sure to put the URL (web address) on the card. Depending on the site, there are return-address labels, letterheads, and even business checks that you can customize.

Create a website.

I suppose you could be in business for a while without a website, but you could be seen as less professional for skipping this step. A simple, attractive website can serve many purposes. It's a handy spot where you (and others who know you) can refer people who want to know more about your business. It is a place to post interesting content about financial topics, testimonials from happy, debt-free clients, and details of upcoming seminars or events you're hosting or attending. It's also a way for people to get your contact information. Your upfront costs will depend entirely on how tech-savvy you are and how much you can do yourself. You might want to hire a marketing company or maybe a freelance page designer and copywriter.

Do-it-yourself entrepreneurs can check out sites like:

- godaddy.com
- webstarts.com
- wix.com
- squarespace.com
- weebly.com

Set up your scheduling software.

I recommend using a scheduling software like Calendly or Acuity (Acuity is our preference) as soon as possible. An online scheduler has a number of benefits. First, it can bring ease to the scheduling process for clients, helping you to avoid the back-and-forth of trying to find times that work for both of you. Second, it offers you built-in boundaries by encouraging you to set hours and honor those hours when clients schedule. Finally, it removes you from administrative tasks early on in your business so you can spend more time coaching.

And of course, you'll need a method for taking credit card payments. Your scheduling software should be able to do this. Your needs will become more sophisticated as your business and tech knowledge grow, but we're starting with the basics to keep costs down.

Some Startup Expenses For Financial Coaches

This list is by no means exhaustive; it's just meant to get you thinking about getting started. Some of the software I recommend offer free versions that can get you going until your business grows and you need more robust versions. You should also budget for talking with an attorney about the types of contracts and agreements you will need for working with clients, as well as how to structure your business and whether you want to incorporate. Talking with a CPA could also be helpful. And your insurance agent can inform you about the types of business insurance (liability, errors and omissions, etc.) that you might want to consider. While consulting with these experts is not required, some coaches prefer to invest in them for the peace of mind.

EXPENSE	MONTHLY AMOUNT	NOTES
Office rent	$0 - $300	• Virtual or home office • Rent small office space (from attorney, CPA, financial advisor) • Coworking space
Additional Training	This needs to be a line item in your budget. You've already invested in this playbook, but what else will you do to learn and grow? The investment you make will depend on a few factors, but it cannot be $0.	After completion of Financial Coach Academy, you may benefit greatly from an online course, small business workshop, or training to utilize the software you'll need. Go get it!
Marketing & Advertising	$150	This can include business cards, flyers, networking lunches, initial website design, or email marketing subscription to name a few.
Website domain	$15 - $40	Costs differ depending on the domain name you choose to purchase.
Liability insurance	$80 - $100	I pay $1K/year for my liability policy.
Credit card processing	$15	I pay $15/month for Paypal.
Other Software • Automate processes • Free up your time • Coach more clients	$50 - $80	I use: • Acuity - for scheduling • Buffer - social media scheduling • JotForm - creating forms • Zoom - online meetings • Zapier - connecting web apps

Commitment Required

In this chapter, I will share some methods for putting "velvet ropes" in place within your business. Each is a way of ensuring that only the best and right kind of client gets past that rope.

You'll soon see why these qualification steps are important. You are assessing the potential client's readiness and commitment levels. You're ensuring that their financial problems or concerns match what you can offer in the way of solutions and that your personalities mesh well enough to be of true service to them.

This advice stems directly from mistakes I made as a new financial coach. If you were to visit my website you might be surprised to see that I don't do free consultations. I used to offer free consultations when I thought that's how you're supposed to do it and hadn't yet questioned whether there was any other way.

As a new financial coach, my free consultation consisted of sitting down with a potential client for an hour or two, asking them about their money, and giving them some advice and guidance at no cost. I hoped that they would be so impressed with the consultation and my coaching that I would easily be able to convert them to long-term clients. What I found was that when I didn't charge for my time and expertise, the prospective clients didn't seem to value it. They came in expecting a sales pitch, so they arrived at our meeting with a wall up.

Other potential clients were no-shows. Or if they did show up, they hadn't completed their prep work. To me, it was even physically obvious that they weren't especially engaged. They slouched in their chairs or sat away from the table. How could I help steer them out of debt if they didn't share any details about that debt? Here I wanted to impress them with my coaching and problem-solving skills, yet the lack of commitment, because it was a free consultation, led to us both being disappointed.

It was terrible. I was miserable and burnt out. I felt like I was giving it my all and the clients weren't. I cared more than they did.

As soon as I stopped doing free consultations, my business dramatically improved. The caliber of client that I attracted improved – and by that, I don't mean their social status or wealth, or their willingness to pay for my services. I mean their readiness level to receive my coaching and to make changes to benefit their own financial health.

Now clients always start with a two-step process: a complimentary Quick Audit phone call and a paid Discovery Session. I get better results, and I make more money. Just as critical, my perspective on my business changed when I stopped giving away my expertise for free.

In short, a certain commitment level is required for people to get the most from financial coaching. Allowing clients to go without making this commitment to change is not serving them well – in fact, it is a disservice to them.

> You're not in the business
> of providing a "quick fix"...

You're not in the business of providing a "quick fix" for money problems, and most folks know that making serious financial changes for growth and improvement is a journey. These changes are not easy, and progress doesn't happen overnight. Your goal is to LEAD the client through the process. You are the expert, and you're going to guide them through it. Do you really want to take on that role for a client who isn't willing to do the work and see it through?

The Quick Audit

When you're first starting out, you're so excited to get a client that you may sometimes forget that your **number one** job at this point is to qualify them – make sure you can help them and that they're a good fit for your services. Are they ready to put in some work, or are they expecting an easy way out of their financial woes?

One way to think about this initial conversation is this: if you are trying to convince them that they need you, **you're doing it wrong**. On the other hand, if you're sharing with them your process and leading them toward their options, you're doing it right.

The Client Journey

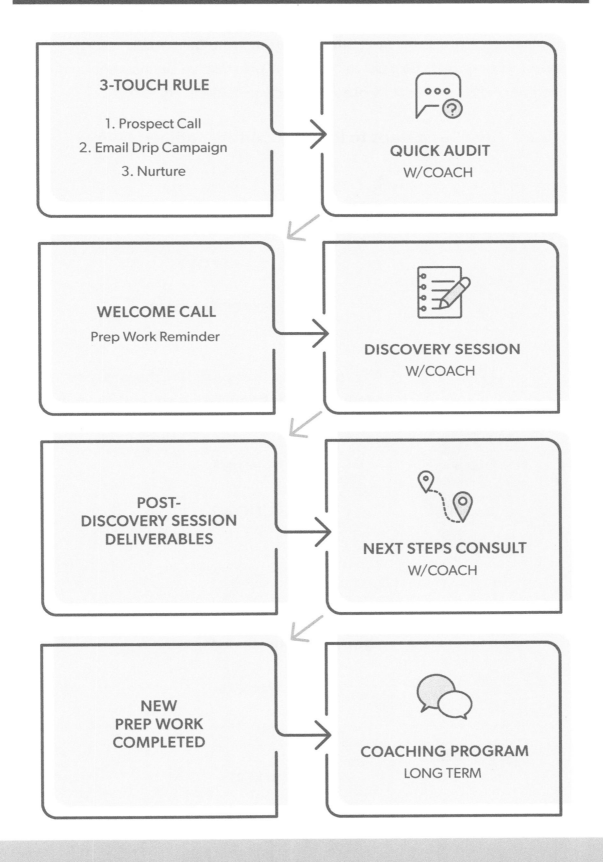

3-TOUCH RULE

1. Prospect Call
2. Email Drip Campaign
3. Nurture

QUICK AUDIT
W/COACH

WELCOME CALL
Prep Work Reminder

DISCOVERY SESSION
W/COACH

POST-DISCOVERY SESSION DELIVERABLES

NEXT STEPS CONSULT
W/COACH

NEW PREP WORK COMPLETED

COACHING PROGRAM
LONG TERM

Learn to be unapologetic when you tell them that this will take some hard work on their part, and that it begins right away. If you're being honest about whether and how you can help them, and what your expectations for them will be, the process will go smoothly.

At Financial Coach Academy, we call this conversation the Quick Audit – short for "quick audition." Its purpose is for YOU to "audition" prospective clients – not for them to audition you – and to schedule those who qualify for a Discovery Session.

There are three basic steps to the Quick Audit, outlined below:

LEAD IN

A friendly introduction.

1. BUILD RAPPORT
2. SET EXPECTATIONS

CREATE DESIRE

Ask questions that pinpoint the prospective client's specific financial issues, and spark their desire to get help with them.

3. PAIN POINT
4. WHY NOW?

GET HIRED

Make the offer such that they are eager to sign up for your services.

5. I CAN HELP
6. OFFER
7. ONBOARD

As a new coach, my recommendation is not to try and perform the Quick Audit when someone calls your business phone and you just so happen to pick up the call. In my experience, this isn't a good idea because preparation and a mental pep talk is often required until you get the hang of it. The Quick Audit is all about taking the lead in the conversation, and getting in the right mindset for the call.

Think about it this way - when we answer the phone we typically say,

> *"Hi, this is Kelsa with Fiscal Fitness, how can I help you?"*

With that question, the prospect is now the driver of the conversation, and it can be much harder to regain control once you've done that. Instead, schedule the call for another time.

You can say something like:

> *"I am so glad you called! I'm heading into a meeting right now. When do you have 20 minutes that I can call you back?"*

Then follow the dialogue for the Quick Audit so you have time to mentally prepare and can take the lead right away.

On your own calendar, block out your Quick Audit as a half-hour – 20 minutes for the call, and a 10-minute buffer afterward, so the conversation can go over if needed without feeling like you have to rush through it. Yet when they schedule, the client will only see a 20-minute call with you. The same goes for the appointment confirmation emails they receive.

On the previous page we introduced the elements of the Quick Audit call. In the next few pages we will review each section in depth.

BUILDING RAPPORT & SETTING EXPECTATIONS

This conversation opener gives you a common connection. It also sets a clear expectation that you have 20-minutes.

> *Hi Tanya,*
>
> *It's Kelsa with Fiscal Fitness. Thank you so much for setting aside these 20 minutes so I can make sure I can help you. I'm curious, how did you hear about me?*

PAIN POINT

This conversation focuses on money right away and reinforces their desire to solve their difficulties with it. It also asks them to tell you about their chief issues.

> *Give me an idea of what problems you're experiencing with your money that you're hoping to solve?*

WHY NOW?

Notice I am not solving the problem OR even offering advice. I'm just saying, *"Yes, I can help."* And I'm trying to see if there's an urgency for them (or not) by asking, *"Why now?"*

> *Those are definitely things I can help with (or not - be honest). I've noticed it can be caused by X, Y, or Z, so we'll want to dig into what might be happening so we can solve it, once and for all. Did something recently happen that sparked the need to solve this, or has it just been building over time?*

I CAN HELP (SESSION VALUE)

Firm up the value of the session before moving onto price. They must see the value in what you're offering before they know the price. The session could cost $5, but if they don't see the value, even $5 is too expensive. Listen and respond to any questions. Once they sound interested, you can move on.

> *I can understand that. I'm going to recommend our Discovery Session. It's a 2-hour, one-on-one session with me. Before the session, my goal is to have you complete prep work so that when you come in, those 2 hours are time focused on strategy. You'll walk away with strategies for overcoming [challenge] and we'll dive into other things such as your financial goals. (Usually, I try to use their own words here, regarding the specific problem they mentioned earlier – such as, 'We devise a plan to... [get you out of debt],' or [put you in control of your spending], etc).*
>
> *My job is to paint a clear picture for you of how to reach those goals. How does the Discovery Session sound?*

OFFER

If they're married or there's another person, the 2nd option is usually best so they can coordinate calendars.

> *We take payment at the time of scheduling, and we recommend you schedule about 10 days out due to the prep work involved. I can get you scheduled right now, or you can go online and see my calendar and book it that way. Which one is easier for you?*

ONBOARD

The Quick Audit either qualifies the client as a great fit for your coaching, or it identifies right away that they may not be. As a result, you either invite them into the process of receiving your help and guidance through the paid Discovery Session, or support them by recommending other resources, professionals, or services that are a better fit. Once the qualified candidate schedules their Discovery Session, begin the process of preparing them for the session so you can effectively coach them.

Fabulous – let's get you scheduled! I'll need your name and phone number, and the email address where you want me to send the prep work.

It's important to say the email address is "where the prep work goes," since they may be inclined to give you a junk email address.

There are just a few things I want to make you aware of before I go to the payment screen, okay?

1) You understand you're going to get prep work, and it's due back to me 48 hours before [date of appointment]? Good, okay!

2) As the meeting gets closer, it's normal to feel nervous and maybe question or doubt coming in, but I do have a very strict cancellation and rescheduling policy – I pretty much don't allow it. I know if you come in, you'll be so glad you did! So, once you schedule this, you're stuck with me – okay?

Be firm about these points, but in a good-natured way.

Perfect! I'm now going to the payment screen, so you'll want to have your debit or credit card handy. (Enter in information you already have and ask for any additional info needed – billing address and credit card information). All right! If I've done everything right, this should go through. (Pause while it's processing…)

The mention of "if I've done everything right..." gives THEM the benefit of the doubt in case the card is declined. It suggests that it was probably your error, which can really help alleviate this awkward moment.

Looks like we're all set! You should receive an email with the prep work provided. Between now and when you come in, don't be a stranger. If you're working through it and not sure, please email or call us, because we're here to help you with it. A good rule of thumb is that you can't over-communicate! If you aren't sure if we need to know something or not, it's better to assume 'yes.'

I am really looking forward to helping you [insert their goal here]. Do you have any more questions for me at this time?

Wonderful. I'll see you in just a couple weeks then, Tanya.

How To Describe Your Coaching Experience

One question you'll get fairly often is, *"How long have you been doing this?"* Or, *"What are your qualifications?"* These may strike fear in the hearts of new financial coaches, but they don't have to – for the most part, they are simply people's basic attempts at conversation.

I've learned to thank them for asking! And I don't define myself by my "official" time as a coach, but by the passion I have for helping people. I often say something like, *"I've been a financial coach since college – I just didn't know it! I've always had an aptitude for personal finance, and started out by helping other kids in my dorm who were drowning in expenses and student debt. I didn't realize I could make a living at it until a few years ago."*

I remember one of the very first networking meetings I ever attended after coaching full-time, and a man asked the inevitable question, *"How long have you been doing this?"* *"Well, just two months full-time,"* I said, *"but I've been doing financial coaching the past four years, sort of as a hobby."* The gentleman looked at me and said, *"You should just say four years; you're being too technical."*

Good point. And from then on, that's exactly what I did!

Look back at your "Why Story" to help you create your own answer to these inevitable questions.

The Client Experience

Now let's look at the second step of this process, the Discovery Session, from the client's point of view. It's safe to say that sharing financial details – especially about debts that outpace income or poor saving and spending habits – is a real emotional rollercoaster ride, and knowing this makes a big difference as a coach.

Your new clients may initially be excited about taking this first step toward cleaning up their financial mess or getting a fresh start. But as the date approaches for their Discovery Session, they're nervous, scared, or embarrassed. And they're finding it all too easy to second-guess their decision to contact you in the first place.

The illustration on page 49 reveals why you need a strict cancellation policy. Setting mine is among the best decisions I've ever made as a financial coach. Clients will want to cancel or push back their Discovery Session. But if we hold them to their commitment, they quickly realize the session is enjoyable and it actually helps them to overcome those worries and fears. So while a policy that says no cancellations and no rescheduling may sound harsh, once I explain to the client that it's in their best interest, it's well-received.

Think about the big decisions in your own life, and you'll realize that people often need help working through their obstacles. Try to think about the Discovery Session as your first opportunity to coach them, get them to open up to you, and learn that they can trust you. And don't be surprised if, at every step of the process, the same worries, thoughts, and anxieties will resurface.

Preparing The Client For Coaching

The goal of the Discovery Session is to provide the client with clarity around their current financial situation along with the action steps and goals to get them where they want to be. In order to accomplish this, I ask the clients to complete prep work in advance of the session. My goal is to make the best use of the time we have with the client during the Discovery Session, so some information-gathering needs to be done ahead of time.

In order to determine what prep work is needed, think back to the SUP2ER Problem you identified in Chapter 1. It's likely most clients will be coming to you for help solving that problem. Ask yourself, *"In order to tackle this problem, what information do I need from the client?"* Then ask yourself, *"Which of those items can I ask for in advance?"* I have two main documents included in my prep work - a questionnaire and a financial worksheet.

Questionnaire

The questionnaire helps me to understand the thoughts and desires of the client. It also helps me gain awareness on what effort and attempts the client has already made in trying to solve this problem. There are details I need to know and others I've learned through experience that I want to know.

What do I *need* to know?

a. Contact details

b. How they're currently managing money

c. What their goals are

I ask this in their prep work, but I also like to have a conversation about it during the session. Posing the question in advance can help the client begin thinking about the future and goals.

d. What they hope to gain from the session

It's likely that as a new coach, you will try to over-deliver during your first few Discovery Sessions. Asking what they hope to gain can help to keep this tendency in check. If you're not careful, over-delivering can actually overwhelm the client, causing them to not take any action.

e. What specific questions or concerns they have

This question helps me to know if I need to do any research or additional work ahead of time.

What would I *like* to know?

f. How they would react if I told them _____?

For example, how would they react if I told them they were in a very tough financial position and drastic changes were needed?

A question such as this helps me to understand how best to deliver tough news and whether I need to sugarcoat my delivery or if they prefer a straight shooter style of advice. How direct or firm can I be with this client?

It's normal for clients to respond with things like *"I'm thinking you will tell me this, please let me down gently."* or *"If that's the case, give it to me straight. I want your expert opinion."*

g. Where do they think they stand financially right now?

Thanks to the Financial Worksheet I have them complete as part of their prep work, I can see the client's financial position before the Discovery Session. I can tell the kind of session we're going to have. This is powerful, but I noticed early on in my coaching career that I would feel anxious in those tough situations. I worried I was about to tell them something they didn't yet know. Asking this question helped me to assess their awareness of their current financial state ahead of time. Including this question in the prep work has had a huge impact on how I feel going into each Discovery Session.

h. When you're inspired, what does it take for you to implement it?

This helps me to gauge in advance what my role as their coach can be. Some clients confess they tend to take a lot of notes, but then stick them in a drawer never to be seen again. I want to ensure that doesn't happen to them with the strategies and changes we discuss during their Discovery Session. Others will say they need time to really think things through before taking action or making changes. Understanding that ahead of time helps me to not throw too much at them all at one time.

Financial Worksheet

My ideal clients come to me because they don't know where their money is going. They yearn for a plan and a clear understanding of what they should or should not be buying. This is the SUP2ER Problem I help my clients overcome during my Discovery Session. As a result, my financial worksheet asks for a detailed list of their income and expenses. Based on the SUP2ER Problem your ideal client faces, what financial data might you need?

How can you gather that in advance? We created a simple Excel or Google Sheets document where the client types in the information and sends it to us. We do not need any sensitive documents by doing it this way. It's client-driven, and while this task is not easy for some clients at this stage, I hear time and time again how valuable this process is for them.

Here is a basic list of what we ask for, keeping in mind you are not limited to just this data:

INCOME

Paycheck amounts, the timing of their pay, sources of income, and any random amounts such as bonuses or commissions.

DISCRETIONARY SPENDING

Estimates for annual expenses like clothing, travel, gifts, and many others.

NECESSARY EXPENSES

Bills and recurring expenses for things like housing, transportation, child care, food, and medical.

DEBT BREAKDOWN

Balances, interest rates, and minimum payment amounts of all debts.

SAVINGS BALANCES & CONTRIBUTIONS

Liquid savings as well as 401(k) or workplace contributions, brokerage accounts, and IRA transfers.

Prep Work Completion

It's important that, soon after the clients receive the prep work to be filled out, they get some kind of friendly nudge from you, ideally by phone. You are asking a lot of them, and not everyone has all their credit card interest rates, balances, and all the details of their financial life – and how they feel about it – neatly rounded up and ready to share.

As they're compiling it, it never hurts to check in, see if they have any questions, and remind them that you'll need the finished forms at least 48 hours in advance of their session. <u>Never apologize for asking for any of this information</u> – and if they complain about it, tell them you need a full picture in order to help them! We also email people one day before their prep work is due – another gentle reminder.

When the prep work comes in, look it over and email the client with any follow-up questions you have. What needs to be clarified? Is anything missing? This also signals that you're doing your part – you're already on the job, thinking about how to help them.

Even if there are no additional questions (which is rare), send a quick email message: *"Thanks for sending in your prep work promptly! We've completed our review and look forward to seeing you."*

Designing Your Discovery Session

One reason I feel completely comfortable charging clients for the Discovery Session is that pulling it together can be a lot of work – and I'm going to deliver a ton of value for their money, but I won't over-deliver and overwhelm or discourage them. They'll leave feeling happy about what they've learned. I know they will feel confident in my ability to understand their issues. Both are critical as we start to work together to conquer their financial pitfalls.

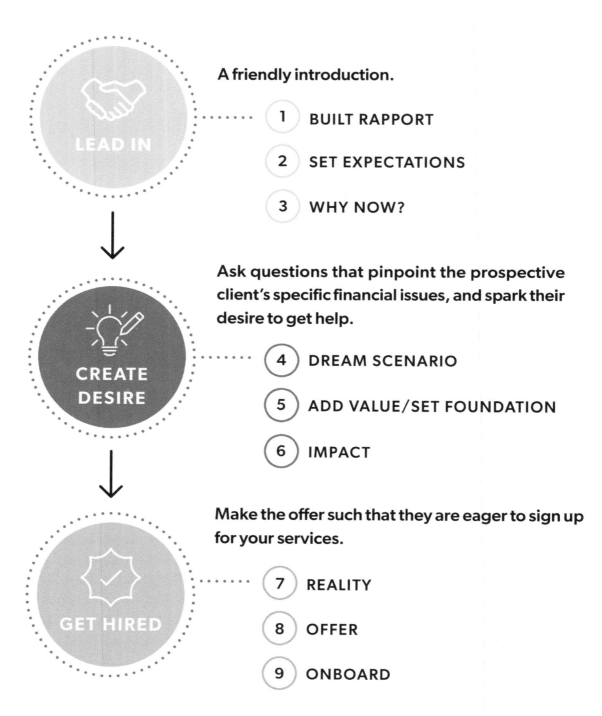

LEAD IN

A friendly introduction.

1. BUILT RAPPORT
2. SET EXPECTATIONS
3. WHY NOW?

CREATE DESIRE

Ask questions that pinpoint the prospective client's specific financial issues, and spark their desire to get help.

4. DREAM SCENARIO
5. ADD VALUE/SET FOUNDATION
6. IMPACT

GET HIRED

Make the offer such that they are eager to sign up for your services.

7. REALITY
8. OFFER
9. ONBOARD

Create the contents and information necessary for your Discovery Session.

What chief problem(s) are you helping a client solve? i.e. credit repair, budgeting, organization, retirement, future planning, mindset, etc.

How much time do you need to solve this problem?
This may be a guess, but shoot for longer at first to give yourself more time. You'll become more efficient. You can always say, *"I allow for two hours just in case, but we don't always need that much time."* That way, it's about the VALUE or RESULT and not the timeframe.

What do you need from the client ahead of time in order to help them solve this problem?

What do you *need* to know?

- ☐ *Contact details.*
- ☐ *How are they currently managing money?*
- ☐ *What are their goals?*
- ☐ *What do they hope to gain from the session?*
- ☐ *What specific questions they have?*

What would you *like* to know?

- ☐ *How would they react if I told them X or Y?*
- ☐ *Where do they think they stand financially right now?*
- ☐ *When you're inspired by something what does it take for you to implement it?*

What will the client gain from this session? What are the results or the benefits to the client from this session?

How can my coaching help them overcome either their mindset or an actual obstacle?

How will the client feel after the session compared to beforehand?

How would you quantify the value of those benefits to the client? What are some direct financial savings they will incur from the session?

Based on this, what is a reasonable price to charge for this session?
Most folks tend to undervalue themselves.

Is this competitive or possible in your market?

What is your hourly rate at this price?   **Does this make you feel uncomfortable?**

Does it cheapen the value you're offering?

What are the deliverables the client will walk away with from the session?

Is there anything you want them to know leading into the session? (expectations)

Brainstorm names for the session.

After I lay out some ideas, strategies and plans for the client, I need to assess where the client is mentally and emotionally so I know how to best move forward. The Discovery Session is valuable by itself but it is rarely possible to solve a lifetime of money habits during one session. At this point in the process, we are just beginning to skim the surface with all this client can accomplish financially. I need to tread carefully and think about whether right now is the appropriate time to bring up next steps or could the idea of more overwhelm the client? To find out, I like to ask them, *"What challenges do you think you'll have with executing these changes?"*

Their response tells me a lot about what our next steps will be.

In my experience, a client is feeling one of three things:

1. Their attitude is, *"I love this conversation, I love the brainstorming we did together, and I want more of it. Tell me how we can continue working together!"*

These are the best kinds of clients of course. They immediately experienced the value I bring to the table and they want more of it. Maybe they could do it on their own but they don't want to. They truly want my guidance and coaching so inviting them to work with me in one of my long-term programs is easy.

2. Their attitude is, *"I've got this! I'm excited! I feel confident that I can make progress on my own and this session has been the best money I have ever spent."*

If my client is on cloud nine, now is not the time to squash that excitement by describing how they need me in order to follow through. I've done my job. I tell them I'll be their biggest cheerleader, and we'll check back with them in about a month to ensure that they're on track for meeting the goals we've laid out in the session. Allowing clients time to attempt the changes on their own will provide valuable insight to both them and you on the role coaching can play going forward.

3. If they are less confident, or seem like they're overwhelmed by the picture I've presented, I let them choose how to proceed. I ask if they would like to try it on their own or if they would like to discuss how coaching can guide them through making these changes. This may go against every sales book you read, but I want them to feel supported and not pressured in their choice. I do not want them to feel obligated to work with me because I have put them under duress.

This is where the gift of empathy can be incredibly powerful. I give them permission to share with me what they're thinking and how they're feeling. I tell them I am here to help if they want it, and we can talk in a day or two after they have had time to sleep on our conversation. I also stress the need for commitment in order to work through their financial challenges and achieve their goals. I invite them to schedule the "Next Steps" consultation call when we can discuss working together more closely so they feel supported in their financial journey.

After the session, every client receives some follow-up deliverables and an email request for feedback. The purpose for the deliverables is that the client will walk away with something tangible to refer back to.

Examples of these deliverables could be:

- Financial report or final budget
- Action list
- Further reading
- Recap/meeting summary

Also following the Discovery Session, clients in the above scenarios 2 and 3 require a follow-up conversation. I call this my "Next Steps" call and it is usually scheduled within a month after the Discovery Session. The purpose is to assess the client's follow through and how they're feeling after attempting the action steps that we co-created. It provides us the opportunity to have a conversation around their needs for long-term coaching. Based on those needs, I can precisely describe the benefits and value of our coaching packages. The legwork of qualifying them has been done and at this stage, they know whether or not they can complete the changes on their own. Therefore, you might think of this appointment as a sales conversation, but it really acts as a check-in call with an invitation to receive more help, with long-term coaching, if and when it's needed. I usually set this to be about 15 minutes.

To summarize, here is the normal flow of a financial coaching client:

QUICK AUDIT PHONE CALL

Qualifies the client and invites them to schedule a paid Discovery Session.

DISCOVERY SESSION

Provides value and solutions to their problems along with a clear and specific action list and an understanding of the challenges they may face when working towards their goals on their own.

NEXT STEPS PHONE CALL

Determines whether more coaching is needed or wanted.

Sales Strategies

We'll cover much more ground on the topic of sales in Chapter 3, but here are a few preliminary points to consider based on what you've learned so far:

Never sell more than one step out. In the Quick Audit, sell ONLY into the Discovery Session. What if someone asks, *"What are the prices after the Discovery Session?"* Tell them you'll talk about that after the Discovery Session if they still need help, but they possibly could only need this session. Always sell into the next step AND ONLY the next step.

The Quick Audit and Next Steps conversations should be more about showing people how they can work with you and inviting them into that process – and not at all about trying to convince someone that they need you.

Ideally, you should strive to create a balanced message in the all-important Discovery Session. Give people a sense of hope and excitement, and don't make the solutions sound too complex or unattainable – but never downplay the obstacles they will face as they work to make these changes in their financial life.

Managing Your Time

You're starting a business, you're developing your programs and their content, you're thinking about marketing, and – oh yeah, you're living your life as well. So, it's time to step back and look at a topic that is critical to all of this: time management.

> If we're time crunched, we're spending more money to buy convenience...

It's amazing how much basic coordination life takes, and people who don't tend to manage their time well also tend not to manage their money well. This makes many things urgent even if they aren't important, as they're inevitably put off until the last minute. And if we're time-crunched, we're also spending more money to buy convenience, from takeout meals to laundry services to housekeeping.

When we budget, we almost always feel like we got a raise – like we have more money – and the same thing is true about time. When time is budgeted and tasks are prioritized and organized, we feel immediately like we have more time each day, and are getting more done.

Gleaned from my own experience as a busy mom, wife, and financial coach – here's a list of tips I've included for effective time management as an entrepreneur:

Make a 10-minute task list.

If you aren't careful, 10 minutes at a time is frittered away here and there because you know it isn't enough to start on one of the bigger items on your to-do list. Resolve not to waste that time! Check email, or listen to a portion of a podcast. Jot some notes for an upcoming session. Research one topic online and bookmark some sites to go back to. Update your budget or check your bank accounts. Unload the dishwasher. Throw in a load of laundry. Make a grocery list. There are hundreds of good uses for that 10-minute time slot. List the ones that you'd like to get done and turn to it whenever you have a small but unscheduled block.

Use an electronic calendar, such as a Google calendar.

This allows you to share and sync your calendar with the other people in your life who need to know or work within your schedule, whether that's an assistant or business partner, a spouse, or other relative. You're less likely to duplicate efforts or schedule competing commitments when you can see everybody's calendar in your immediate orbit, and they can see yours.

Time-block your calendar.

Every Sunday, I sit down and time-block my upcoming week – that is, select blocks of time each day, decide what I need to do that day, and schedule those items in blocks. How much time for a "block?" Start with 30-minute increments. Until you get used to scheduling this way and trusting your commitment to your schedule, shorter blocks are good beginnings. (My personal ideal block is 90 minutes, but for some topics, 30 might not be enough, 60 might be fine. I've heard that Tesla founder Elon Musk blocks his time in 5-minute increments!)

Customize your calendar to inspire you.

You can color-code your electronic calendar based on the overall category of the items (family time, content creation, marketing, etc.), which also allows you to easily see at a glance what you might not be doing enough of. Be creative with what you call certain time blocks to make them meaningful or motivational for you. (For instance, I think "Marketing" seems like a dull title for my outreach efforts, so I call those time blocks "Engagement." That's what works for me.)

Put a lot to accomplish into a time block.

Lump or "batch" projects of a similar nature together. Have you noticed that if you give yourself an hour to work on one thing, it will take an hour? And if you give yourself two hours to do it, it will take two hours? Pile multiple, related tasks into that time block and you will find it's better to have too much to do in the allotted time than not enough. Nobody says you have to finish it all in that block, either.

Don't forget to block off some free time.

Yes, you're planning for time to not plan! For 30 minutes or an hour, I can do whatever I want. This doesn't necessarily mean taking time off – it's free time. If you want to watch Netflix or take a walk, terrific. But you could also work on your business or catch up on phone calls. It gives you some freedom, and you've built some flexibility into your schedule.

Put a routine in place.

Sure, life gets crazy sometimes. Michael and I are more supportive of each other when we are aware of *how* busy we are and *what* we have going on. This helps in terms of budgeting because we can see which calendar items have costs associated with them, from haircuts to the dog groomer, to doctor visits. We can decide together if, on a very busy week, we might eat out or budget less for that week's groceries.

Create a schedule and stick to it.

I have one day a week that I use for priorities other than client sessions. You might choose instead to schedule an hour or two, on multiple days a week. Building time in early to work on the business is one of the best tips I can recommend to you.

Think about your natural energy levels.

You know which times of day you're the most creative, hungriest, sleepiest, or most scattered. Time-block the hardest projects when you are the best at problem-solving or brainstorming. Don't plan something big at a time when you're usually at a low energy point in your day.

Create folders for your internet bookmarks.
The folders should share the same names as your time blocks, and should contain all the online sites you've bookmarked for reference on related subjects. During a particular time block, limit yourself to ONLY go into that folder. When I'm supposed to be working on "Content Creation," I cannot go to my "Social" file and catch up with friends on Facebook! This system helps manage your own self-expectations.

 If it's not a 'Hell, yes!' – it's a no.
If someone asks you to do something and your first reaction isn't natural enthusiasm, say no unless it's something you really want to do. If your time is limited, the things that would prompt a hearty, 'Hell, yes!' should be your priorities. As a business owner, it's common to find yourself working on something you don't necessarily enjoy, especially at first. But these provide a great list for tasks that could or should be delegated or outsourced as quickly as possible.

If you're not using any of these time management strategies at the moment, start by planning only one day ahead. The more you learn to trust yourself that you're going to follow through on just that day, the easier it will become to plan one week out.

> The goal is progress,
> not perfection...

My mantra for time management is the same as for budgeting: *"The goal is progress, not perfection."* If you can plan for 75 percent of what's going to come up in your financial life, then the other 25 percent will be easier to tackle. The same is true for time. By planning much of your time to accomplish what you truly want to do, you'll be clearing the way for the unexpected and inevitable interruptions (good and bad) that crop up – and can seamlessly get back on track when they do.

Chapter 02

Action Summary

☐ **1. Construct your professional first impression:**

    a. Create your business name.

    b. Buy a web-domain.

    c. Set up Google Suites or other email service.

    d. Set up Google Voice or other phone line.

    e. Create an email signature and voicemail greeting.

    f.   Print some business cards.

    g. Create a basic website.

    h. Establish a scheduling software account to use.

☐ **2. Write out your beginner's business budget.**

☐ **3. Devise your Quick Audit script and practice it with a colleague or friend.**

    a. Set up a template for a 20-minute appointment (don't forget a title for the appointment, confirmation text, and a reminder.)

    b. Write the Quick Audit script and practice it with a colleague or friend.

☐ **4. Identify and create pre-session materials.**

    a. Set up a template for a Discovery Session appointment (don't forget a title for the appointment, confirmation text, and a reminder.)

    b. Establish price; set up a payment processing through a Stripe or Paypal.

    c. Identify and create pre-session materials.

    d. Rehearse the session flow with a colleague or friend.

    e. Identify and create post-session deliverables.

☐ **5. Employ some time management strategies for yourself and your business.**

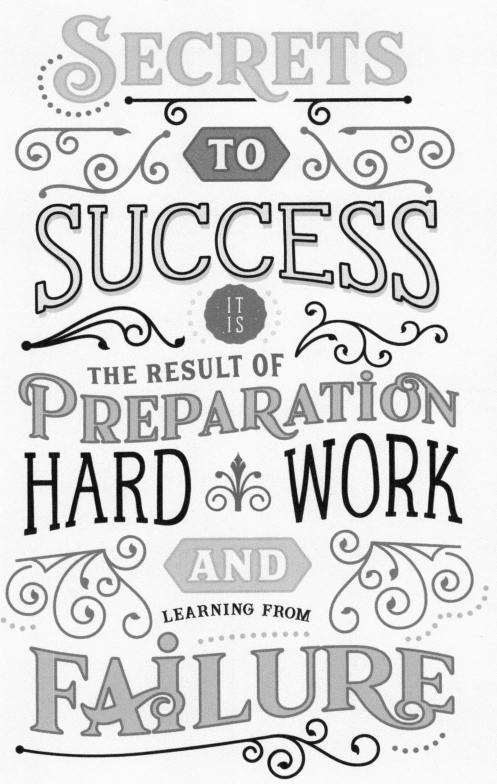

THERE ARE NO SECRETS TO SUCCESS IT IS THE RESULT OF PREPARATION HARD WORK AND LEARNING FROM FAILURE

• COLIN POWELL •

Knowing how to respond to the different scenarios that a potential client might have, understanding common objections and improving my confidence in how to overcome them was so valuable. This really gave me the confidence I needed to show potential clients why they should work with me and dismiss the imposter syndrome.

KACY SMITH

STRAIGHT CENTS

Chapter 03

Selling With Integrity

You didn't decide to become a financial coach to go into sales. However, sales are a necessary part of your business – and for your clients' sake, you'll want to learn, grow, and challenge yourself to become more proficient at selling.

When I began financial coaching, I was terrible at sales conversations – I didn't even know how to begin reconciling some of the questions and objections I received. I shied away from the sales part of the conversation and even left some of my clients hanging at the end of our Discovery Sessions when I'm sure they could have used more help from me.

> ... your true belief in the value you offer will make all the difference.

It isn't only about having the sales conversations for the sake of making the sale. You first need to focus on your own mindset around these conversations and initiate them with integrity and conviction. Not everyone is comfortable with selling, and your true belief in the value you offer will make all the difference.

In the last chapter, we walked through a Discovery Session – your first shot at really helping someone. At the end of that session, you'll have an opportunity to invite the client into a longer-term commitment with you. This is where the sales skills and confidence will serve you well. So, let's work on them! This chapter is focused on breaking down objections on the spot, as they arise, and learning how to keep the conversation flowing naturally. I'll even share some key phrases, scripts, and break it down step-by-step.

To be skillful at sales, you have to do some work on yourself. Do you really believe in the value of financial coaching? Can you describe those beliefs, and share them sincerely with others? Do you believe that some of the objections you'll hear are valid, even though you'll have good answers for them?

It's easier to have a sales conversation when you know how well your coaching will overcome whatever obstacle you encounter. Don't just take my words from this chapter and quote them or memorize them – you'll want to adapt them, paraphrase them, and make them fit your own values and beliefs.

Developing Your Sales Mindset

Developing your sales mindset is a continuous process that involves being mindful during each client conversation. I'm still adapting my sales process, based on my observations of a client's reactions and body language. Are they leaning in and showing interest, or leaning back and zoning out? How do I feel during our discussion? Active listening and critical thinking skills are required.

You might realize it isn't about sales at all – it might be your marketing efforts that need tweaking, to attract a different type of client in the first place. As we discussed in Chapter 1, if you have the wrong client sitting in front of you, you've already set yourself up to fail. That isn't a sales problem. That's a marketing problem.

One pitfall I see with new coaches is that they focus on all the tools they're giving to the client – the budget, the templates, the handouts. I want you to believe instead that YOU are the ultimate value-add. Your coaching is what will give them the knowledge to move forward and use these tools effectively. The tools are great, but you're the prize.

The language you use in your session can reinforce this:

> You'll know what to do – but doing it is a whole new ball game.
>
> The steps are simple, but that doesn't mean they're easy.

Another natural concern of new coaches is rejection. Rejection isn't fun, and you will experience it sometimes. What you need is a clear decision, and the way to get it is by confidently asking direct questions. Otherwise, the client will give "soft no's" about moving forward. These "soft no's" can feel like death by a thousand paper cuts. Each subtle rejection creates self doubt and only prolongs the rejection. The coach then internalizes the client's indifference and starts to worry: *"What am I doing wrong? What else should I say?"*

Wouldn't you rather hear an honest, "No, thanks," and be able to move on? The converse is investing time and energy into a client who isn't interested and isn't sure how to tell you that because you haven't asked a direct question.

Take a deep breath and observe yourself. Does your voice change, or speed up, when you transition into the sales conversation? Does your eye contact change? Almost everyone experiences at least one of these. Sales is where your confidence in your own skills must come to the forefront. The trust you have in your own value and benefits will have to shine.

Sales isn't easy, but it's necessary for your clients to get the results they need – and for you to make your coaching business succeed.

Sales Questions To Consider

How do I feel when someone is trying to sell me something?

For me, what makes a sales pitch a positive experience rather than a negative one?

As the customer, what are my biggest fears during sales conversations?

As the person doing the selling, what are my biggest fears during sales conversations?

Why is it important for me to lead with courage during the sales conversation?

For the client, what are the benefits of having me lead sales conversations with courage?

What are some simple steps I can take to prepare myself for the sales aspect of each client conversation?

Teeing Up The Sales Conversation

One way you can ensure the sales conversation goes smoothly is to establish or tee up the value of what you offer during the entire Discovery Session. Plant seeds throughout the session that indicate your willingness to work further with the client on their financial concerns. It shouldn't be all coaching until the last ten minutes, when you pivot into some kind of "hard-sell" mode to get them to sign up for more. No drama needed here! It should be a subtle mix at all times, which builds their trust in you and gets them thinking naturally about how they'd benefit from continuing to work with you.

Before you head into a Discovery Session, with the client's financial prep work in hand, you'll have a pretty good idea of what you might be able to accomplish with them during this single session. Think about the ways you can support them if they decide to move forward with future coaching, so you can add those prompts into your Discovery Session. For example, you may solve their most immediate problem, but more coaching will help them tackle what comes next. As their coach, you'll likely be more aware of this than they are, so in advance of the session, think through ways you can plant these seeds.

Here are several points at which these prompts are most effective:

On the Prep Form:

- *"Are you interested in discussing future coaching services?"*

- *"When you feel inspired by something, what does it take for you to implement it?"*

In the Discovery Session, you can refer to their answers in pointing to the need for some follow-up to help them follow through with your suggestions.

Questions about where they see themselves:

- *"What is your ultimate goal with your money?"*

- *"What is it that you're hoping to accomplish with a financial coach?"*

You surely can't meet these big goals or solve every problem in a single session – but you can discuss how you've moved them forward and point out that future coaching will bridge the gap.

Again, you're planting seeds:

"I know you want to be here (_____ big goal _____).
We can definitely get you there with some future coaching – but today we're going to concentrate on the first or second step toward that goal."

During the Discovery Session

As you and the client are talking, you'll no doubt be taking notes. At the top of my page, I jot down some specific points or phrases I'm hearing from the client that I'll be able to use later in the sales conversation at the end of the session.

Keep track of time so you'll be sure to end 15 to 20 minutes early, to give you time for the sales discussion. You don't want to have to rush at the end. The client is looking to you to guide the conversation. From the moment the session begins, you already know you plan to end with the sales conversation, and it will flow more naturally if you are well prepared for it. Rehearse if you need to, using their initial responses to the questionnaire.

It's normal to have part of your brain playing devil's advocate during the sales conversation – that voice in your head that says, *"Oh, don't be pushy!"* Or, *"Well, this is gonna be awkward…"* So as you rehearse – or even just before an actual sales conversation – take a moment to give this voice a more positive approach. Think, *"This is when I get to invite this client to really experience the good stuff!"* *"This is when we get to talk about making massive improvements in this person's life, for the long term."*

Create a Sense of Urgency:

Create an impressive timeline for them and reinforce it. This alludes to more steps you can take with them.

→

"When I create the Ultimate Financial Power Plan, people get results so much faster because they can see their money so much more clearly."

Use phrases like:	→	*"We help clients see dramatic results," or, "The speed at which you will get results is greater."*

- -

Give them specific milestones to meet. With this language, the clients who don't meet the deadlines can't help but wonder if they need more coaching to help them move forward.	→	*"I would want to see that done in the next 30 days, and this item done in the first 45 days – and if we were to work together, that's what I would help you to achieve – so, that's the deadline I want you to create for yourself."*

- -

Part of your coaching is stressing personal accountability. Be direct about your expectations that the clients will do their part because they're committed – not to a single session, but to the process.	→	*"That's the timeline you want to put in place for yourself."*

- -

Focus on the *How* by giving the client actions and takeaways, while also understanding there is more to come.	→	*"These are the things we need to do right away, but these are immediate steps, not the only steps."*

- -

The Discovery Session simply can't cover everything they need to do, forever. These are the steps required to build a strong foundation. Of course, we want to do more! But for now, we're starting with the foundation.

Reinforce the Inherent Value in Your Coaching:

Stress that this single session isn't all you can do for them.

$\rightarrow$

"Later when we talk about moving forward, it's something I can create for you if that's something you want us to do."

Mention your oversight role.

$\rightarrow$

"I would hold you accountable to these deadlines. I am going to keep this top-of-mind for you. I can help to keep you focused."

Help them to recognize and experience the growth they will see as a result of taking these steps. Share the emotional perspective.

$\rightarrow$

"When you make this change, here are some of the things you'll likely experience, think, or feel at that time. Here's what might come up when you do that. My job is to help you through those growing pains. So when they happen, you don't want to quit."

Acknowledge that change is hard and you're here with a steady hand to help them navigate it.

$\rightarrow$

"When you make these changes, there's likely a time when you will want to quit. Not all the changes we implement will go smoothly. Not all will occur quickly, get immediate results – or even the ideal results we're shooting for. My job is to help you see that not all hope is lost; that we're still moving forward, and we'll find other things for us to do during the process that we're not seeing right now."

Tout your experience. $\rightarrow$ *"In the first 30 days (or few months), I know what problems, hurdles, and obstacles you will face. My job is to help you move past those obstacles."*

The goal here is to be positive and realistic at the same time. Don't downplay how challenging it will be. They will feel growing pains. Reassure them that if they start to have challenges, you're here to help, while also holding them accountable to the actions and monitoring the results.

Compare the Value You Offer Today Versus the Future

This indicates that in the future, there will be things you can work on together – but this first session is focused on items for them to accomplish. $\rightarrow$ *"The goal of this session is to give you the action items to complete on your own."*

The message is:
'You will likely need my expertise in the future, and I'll be here for you.' $\rightarrow$ *"I know what I'm describing to you sounds simple. My job is to take really complex or overwhelming concepts and ideas and make them simple for people, and I love that I can do that so well. But if I'm not careful, I'm going to make you think this will be super-easy for you. In fact, some of these steps will be hard, and you could have some real challenges accomplishing them."*

As I first mentioned in Chapter 2, the Discovery Session is a delicate balance between giving people hope, excitement, and empowerment, while also being clear about the obstacles they will face as they try to make these changes. Helping them meet these challenges and work around the obstacles is exactly how you will continue to add value as their financial coach.

> "Selling is really about having conversations with people and helping improve their company or their life."
>
> - LORI RICHARDSON, SALES SPEAKER & TRAINER

How The Client Conversation Works

It's important to understand how the conversation tends to flow for the sales portion of the Discovery Session. You have provided the client with a number of action steps, and you have just finished summarizing the key takeaways of the meeting. Hopefully, you have about 15 to 20 minutes remaining.

From there, here is a typical exchange, with some notes about what each step might signal to you as the financial coach:

Coach:
"What challenges do you think you'll face in making all of these changes?"

Client mentions a challenge:
Time constraints, confusion, overwhelmed, etc.

Coach:
"You have some options for us continuing to work together where I can help you with (said challenge). Could I share those with you now?"

Client hopefully says yes.

If they say they're not interested, do not try to convince them they should be. Respect that! But you'll find that most people say yes.

Coach:

Describe the key benefits the client would achieve working with you for the next 3-6 months. Do not describe ALL the benefits of working with you – focus on the 2-3 that are most significant knowing what you know about this client. This is where the notes you've taken will be helpful.

Coach: *"I would love to continue this work with you. How does this sound to you?"*

During this time, do not discuss price or number of sessions. Those details don't matter yet. First, you must confirm that the client sees the value in what you're proposing. The goal is to confirm that they are interested before moving forward in the conversation. You need to find out if what you're describing sounds worthwhile to them.

Client may say, *"This sounds great!"*

Then, you can dive into specifics such as price, number of sessions, and so on, and that's when you might encounter some objections.

If so, continue to discuss price, logistics, etc., and field objections. If not, ask what they would hope to achieve that you might have missed – maybe it's something you just didn't mention, but they would definitely gain from knowing more about. Perhaps it will make the difference in deciding to sign up for a program.

But they must first see the value in the program and in working with you. Otherwise, no price will be worth it.

Responding To Questions Or Concerns

You'll get a lot of questions as a coach, and how you answer them will affect how much time you spend on each client's case and whether you ultimately think it is time well spent. Here are a few queries that could be interpreted as objections – which I think strike fear in the hearts of newer financial coaches – with notes about how I deal with them. Not everyone will agree with my approach, but these should at least get you thinking about how you would handle them.

- (?) -

QUESTION: *"Can I call (or email) you and ask questions?"*

Background: What I find is, the small questions that come up are actually connected to much bigger problems – it isn't usually only one piece that's missing. And if I haven't worked with this client for a few months, I have no idea what their full, current picture is. Has anything major changed? One snafu is oftentimes the sign of other things going on, and I can't typically solve anything without diving in deeper. I can't troubleshoot the puzzle when I can't see all the pieces.

The point of the Discovery Session is to give the client an action list to implement on their own. Some are able to do things on their own; others need my ongoing support – but it's one or the other. You don't tiptoe in and keep asking for additional help, free of charge.

What I tell the client: "I reserve answering questions for individuals who continue on in a program with me. If I allow you to email me, then it's likely I'm enabling you. I want to see you make all of these changes. I want to see you make a total transformation with your money – and because one obstacle is typically attached to others, if we move forward, I want to have my hands on all these pieces, not just one piece of it."

- (?) -

QUESTION: *"Why is your fee so high?"* (This might also be a statement: *"Your fee is too high."*)

Background: Everyone has heard, 'You get what you pay for.' Don't shy away from that – own it! You're providing a valuable service. Do not apologize. People are most likely to voice price concerns because we have not clearly articulated the value we offer or what they will gain from working with us. In other words, this ends up being a value-related question, not a price-related question.

What I tell the client: *"I understand my fee is an investment. By questioning it, that tells me I haven't done a good enough job sharing with you what we would accomplish together during this time. So, let's take a step back and discuss that a bit more."*

· (!) ·

STATEMENT: *"If you really help them, you should be able to help them enough that they don't need to pay for you on a credit card."*

A statement like this usually comes from someone other than a potential client.

Background: If I had to always find enough money in their budget specifically to pay my fee, I could make them cut things that I know are important to them, simply to justify my fee. In fact, I believe that's putting way too much ownership on the coach in this process, and not enough on the client. Coaching is a two-way relationship, and the client is the actual owner.

The client has agreed to pay for coaching services, which typically last for a short time and are paid for within that time period. However, the benefits they'll receive from coaching are long-lasting and will be useful for the rest of their lives. I know and believe that I can change people's lives – but I don't have a lifetime to charge them for what I can do for them in that short time period.

How do you reconcile this as a coach? It's really challenging. Believe that you are worth it to them, even if they have to put your fee on a credit card or take money out of savings to pay you.

What I tell this person: *"I believe in the results I get for my clients, and while most of those are financial in nature, even more importantly, my clients feel better. They're happier, they sleep better, they have a lot less stress, they feel more in control, and they're setting goals and achieving them. And it's up to the client to decide if it is worth a credit card charge that may take a few months to pay off or a one-time dip into a savings account."*

Remember, you won't field every one of these questions in a single conversation – thank heavens!

· ·

Helpful Phrases For Client Conversations

*"You will **know** what to do – but **doing** it is a whole new ball game. The steps are SIMPLE, but that doesn't mean they're EASY."*

"Later, when we talk about moving forward..."

"While we tackle things weekly, let's make sure it is at a pace you are comfortable with. My job is to challenge you, but I'm not going to make you do anything you're not comfortable with."

"Let's dive into how we can make this happen for you."

"I would love to work with you."
(Do not fear that this feeling won't be reciprocated. Own it!)

Inviting The Objections

The things most of us do to avoid rejection are amazing. Here's an interesting approach – why not invite people to tell you what they're most afraid of, or why they're hesitating during the sales conversation? Don't be afraid to hear what they have to say!

You might ask:

What is your biggest fear when making these changes?

(This is where you'll hear people say, 'I can't do it.' Or, 'I won't be able to do it.')

What challenges do you think you'll face when trying to make all these changes?

Right now, are you more concerned with the financial aspect of this program or the time commitment?

Try an open-ended question that invites a response:

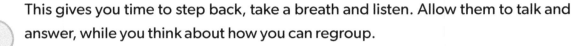

- *What do you think of that?*
- *Tell me why you think that. Let's talk about it.*

This gives you time to step back, take a breath and listen. Allow them to talk and answer, while you think about how you can regroup.

- *What would happen if, in four months you had money in your savings accounts, you were making progress on your debt, you had clarity on your finances, and (X amount) went on a credit card to pay for this? How would you feel? What impact would that have for you? Where would you be if we did that?*

Or ask 'yes or no' questions:

- *Does this sound valuable to you right now?*
- *Does this sound like something that would benefit you?*
- *Does this sound like a good fit for what you're looking for?*

Here's a keen observation you can make when a person's answers to these questions indicate a lack of confidence in their own ability to dig themselves out of their financial pit:

"Your fear of failing at something with your finances is a mindset around money that I would love to help you overcome. I want you to feel confident in your ability to experiment, and to enjoy your money and trust that no matter what happens, you can handle it financially. But that's something we'll have to work on, because we can't make that change overnight."

And if they tell you they don't think they'll have the time for the work and follow-through this is going to take, here's one possible approach:

"My job as your coach is to support you in making these changes and in following through on what you say you want to do – to make these changes and not procrastinate. I want to help you keep this a priority for yourself. I understand you want to look at the schedule, but this may be one of the very first ways that I'm going to coach you – by not letting you move this to the back burner, and not letting fear or worry stop you from moving forward."

This exercise will help you identify real objections you may hear and assist you in creating a response with integrity.

What is the objection I am likely to hear?

Is this a mental block the client is having or a real and valid objection?

How can my coaching help them overcome this hurdle?

If the objection is valid, are they likely to make the changes without you? Explain.

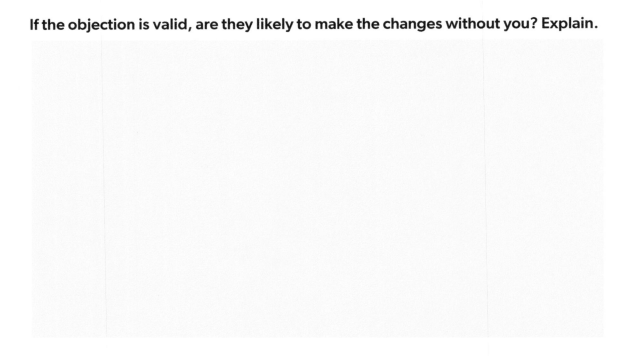

Moving Forward After The Discovery Session

Now let's look at a few different situations in which you've sat down with the client(s) and had your Discovery Session. You're wrapping things up and thinking about next steps.

 The client says, 'I feel good about what you've presented!'

Don't leave things open-ended. Get their follow-up call scheduled right then and there:

> *"Let's schedule a 15-minute call 30 days from now, so I can check in on you and make sure you are getting the types of results I know you should be getting at that point."* It isn't another question-and-answer session – it's a checkup call. *"In 30 days, you should be feeling very different about your money, so I want to make sure that's happening."*

The idea is that while the client may not hire you for ongoing coaching, they will be a walking talking testimonial for you. They will rave about you, tell others about their experience, and will serve as an ambassador for you and your business. To create an ambassador for yourself, you can say something like: *"I'm so glad these two hours had this big of an impact for you!"*

Plant a seed for the future:

> *"It's normal that whatever we conquer in this session, as we grow, we will come up with a whole new set of obstacles we weren't aware of. I hope you'll give me the pleasure of working with you again at some point if that does happen."*

Privately, ask yourself whether this client is going to continue to struggle without you.

Do you think the person will execute the plan exactly as you've laid out, and all the money is going to go toward their goals without you?

If you aren't sure this client can really do it, share your concerns:

> *"I'm torn right now. I'm seeing that the only way for us to work together is if you pause some of your goals and use those funds to pay for my ongoing help in the coming few months. You really may be able to do this on your own, but I'm not sure. So, I'd like to see you try it for a month, and let's schedule a phone call for a month from now, to see if you're executing everything beautifully. By then, if you haven't been able to manage it, do you see how it might be worth it to put your goals on pause for four months, so we can put this solid system in place and to set you up for success? That's what I'd like to talk about with you a month from now. So for now, it's 'do or die' time."*

There's nothing worse than not pushing and not being transparent and honest about it – and then, hearing a few months later that they didn't do anything and they're still exactly where they were when they came to see you.

Think about what is in service of the clients. These conversations may not be easy, but it's worth a little discomfort on your end and crucial for them to get the results they need.

. . . .

 The client says, "I'm good! But this is enough."

If you hear, 'This is good, I feel good about these first steps and this is enough,' it means they don't want more coaching. This isn't because they dislike you or what you've done – they may be impressed with what you've laid out for them and anxious to get started on making the changes, or are content with solving the immediate problem. But they're not interested in doing more than that.

One way this shows up is with statements like, *"I'm not ready for all that."*

This reaction also often indicates that they're not a good fit for you as a long-term client. It's a red flag that they're not ready for coaching. Wouldn't you rather have that information now than later? Be kind and supportive – but it's okay to let them opt out if you feel yourself trying to convince them that they need more, or should want more, when they don't.

. . . .

 The client loved the session and wants to move forward, but has objections.

The goal of discussing a client's objections is not to talk them into working with you. What's usually happening in the client's mind is, they aren't sure they're really ready for the next steps, or they aren't sure they can succeed. You've given them a lot of information, and they need time to process it before making any big decisions.

. . . .

And you might hear...

 "I have to talk to my husband/wife/partner."

Sometimes this is valid and other times, it's a way for them not to commit. Your goal is to ask some deeper questions and encourage a follow-up phone call. Ask...

- *Overall do you feel like your husband/wife/partner supports you in the endeavors that you want to make in your life?*

- *If your husband/wife/partner knew that you could spend money to solve the problems we've been working through, do you think they would say no to that?*

- *What if we scheduled a time right now when I can hop on a call with you and your husband/wife/partner, so I can answer any questions they have and I can share what I'm hoping to help you with?* (Don't leave it up to them to have a conversation with their significant other and get back to you.)

- *What do you think they're going to say? What objections do you think you'll hear from them?*

. . . .

 "It's overwhelming."

This typically means the person is a bit confused or indecisive and likely isn't taking action because they don't know what to do first.

Possible responses:

- *I know I just threw a lot at you, and one way I can support you is that, instead of saying, 'Here's everything I want you to accomplish in the next 30 days, 6 months, and even maybe 1 year of your life,' by working with me, I actually help you break it down into weekly action items and I'm going to help you create baby steps.*

- *Instead of leaving here feeling overwhelmed, let's talk about how I can support you in making these changes going forward, and how we can make this feel more manageable for you.*

. . . .

"I'm too busy."

Time management and money management go hand in hand, and the person who, until now, hasn't made the time to sort out their financial picture really does need your help.

Possible response:

- *That's certainly a problem because managing your money, setting goals, putting a system in place that allows you to make amazing decisions with your money will require time. How much time do you think you could dedicate to this process each week?*

. . . .

" I don't want to put coaching on a credit card."

When a person has been adding recent charges to their credit card prior to coming in – whether it's for a vacation or car repair or Christmas gifts – to say coaching doesn't belong on that card is simply not a valid excuse. Those items were obviously important enough for them to pay for on credit, and even if they didn't feel great about it at the time, that's what they allowed themselves to do.

Possible response:

- *In the last few months, you've added things to your credit card – and this could be the very last thing you ever add to your card balance. The items that you charged were somehow important enough to you that you went into debt to get them. Now, if you're sincerely ready to make these changes and you want my help, using the card one more time might be the step we need to take.*

- *There might be a way to put only a portion of the fee on your credit card. I'll check your budget (or let's look at your budget) and see if we can find a way to minimize what goes onto the card.*

. . . .

 "Putting it on my credit card will hurt my credit score."

Possible response:

- *"Are the long-term results you want to achieve worth the drop of a few points with your credit report for a short period of time?"*

If they say 'no,' that's a bigger issue, which calls for a value-based conversation. You might say: *"I think the emphasis on the credit score is a red flag to me; you may be attaching too much of your self-worth to it, based on what I'm hearing; and I'd love to dive more into that with you. I would rather have you feel really empowered by the fact that you're setting and accomplishing goals with your money, rather than focus on how you should feel about your money based on your credit score. So again, that's a big red flag to me."*

Navigating The Ultimate Objection

It may be the simplest – and yet the most complex – of all the hesitations or objections you'll hear as a financial coach:

- *"You can see in my budget that I can't afford this." "This sounds great, but I'm sure I can't afford it." "Yeah, but how am I going to pay for it?"*

These types of statements indicate the client is building a defensive wall around this transaction, which often is the result of their own sense of embarrassment. They don't want to offend you by flat-out saying they can't afford you, and they probably feel badly about it.

Your job here is to first decide if they really can commit and want to move forward, or if they're making excuses because they have no intention of agreeing to further coaching.

This means asking questions like:

- *"If you can find a way to make this short-term investment worthwhile for you – meaning that the immediate and long-term impacts outweigh the short-term cost – would you want to move forward?"*

- *"If we could find a way to make this short-term investment feel better to you and we can see what the impact is, would you want to move forward?"*

The client might be feeling tense, afraid, anxious, nervous, or self-conscious – or any combination thereof. They might even feel bad about themselves because they genuinely want the coaching assistance, but they've been down this road so many times and are ready to concede with a sigh, *"Here I am again, wanting something I can't afford."*

Don't tiptoe around it or shy away from it. Depending on what you hear, you can allay their fears and address some of their specific concerns by being positive and realistic.

- *Let's dive in to see how we can make this happen for you.*

- *I'm glad you brought that up. Let's take a look at your budget and see what this looks like.*

- *I love problem-solving around money for any decision you have in front of you – it just so happens to be my coaching you're evaluating at the moment! But just know that, going forward, whatever you're facing financially, we're going to tackle it in a very similar fashion, okay?*

- *I know you've probably felt like there are things in your life you've wanted for yourself that you haven't been able to afford, and I know how that feels, so let's see if we can make this possible for you. I want you to see that whatever you want, we're going to try and find a way to afford it. The first time we're going to do it with me as your coach just so happens to be around hiring me.*

- *If you want to work together, let's figure this out. How can we make this happen for you?*

If a client's budget is truly break even and the decision to hire you comes down solely to cost, carve out more time than usual for the sales conversation, perhaps an extra 20 or 30 minutes. Don't rush it. If you don't get through all of it, say, *"We're out of time today, but I really want to continue this conversation. I want to help you feel confident in making this decision about moving forward. Let's schedule a 30-minute conversation for tomorrow so we can pick up where we left off and see how we can work together."*

DO NOT OFFER A DISCOUNT…
unless there's a very compelling reason – perhaps for a military family, or a "friends and family" discount. Cutting the price as a bargaining tool has the side effect of devaluing your services and your expertise. It also can make you appear desperate.

Now that you've offered to help them figure out how to come up with the money, it's time to take another look at their financial picture based on the budget information they've given you for the Discovery Session. For you, the bonus benefit here is that you're actually strengthening their belief in the value of your coaching as you do this.

Steps For Finding Money In A Tight Budget

At the end of the Discovery Session, ideally there will be enough time to check the client's budget figures and discuss where the money will come from for your coaching services. If not, it's important to schedule time within the next day or two to have this discussion.

When evaluating their expenses and trying to find money to pay for the coaching, sometimes we can find the entire fee – let's say it's $499 per month – but sometimes, we'll find only $300 and then other options can be examined. As you review expenses and make suggestions, keep in mind - people don't need to say 'yes' to all of them. However, if their goal is to not put it on a credit card, you can explain their options and encourage them to pick and choose.

 Take a closer look at the client's budget.
Since we know this is a short-term investment, we're going to look at the budget to see first if we can afford it, and decide how much of it we can afford. If the fee is $500/month, for instance, and they have $200 extra, we only need to find the $300 difference.

 Discuss what they're willing to give up.
The first thing we're going to do is simply ask the client, *"What can you give up – just for the next four months – because this is important to you?"* Since we know it's a short-term investment, we're going to look at the budget and help them decide what they could give up or cut back, for a short period of time, because we know the long-term benefits and impact it's going to have are worth it. *"Let's see how, together, we can make it happen."*

 Pinpoint any "extra" amounts that could be temporarily redirected.
These likely are going to a goal, such as paying down debt or buying a home. For the next four months only, that extra could go toward this $500. Would the client

commit to making a minimum payment to a credit card instead of the higher payment, for a short, fixed time period? I might tell them, *"You don't feel like you have the extra cash right now, but I know I'm going to find it if we move forward – and all we're saying is that, for the next four months, it's going to go to this financial coaching, because making these changes is your goal."*

 Consider withdrawing "small amounts from small buckets."
During my Discovery Session, I often recommend that the client sets up savings accounts for non-recurring expenses such as clothing, gifts, travel, etc. People in need of financial coaching aren't often saving much, so we could take $50 each from five accounts without having a major budgetary impact.

Ask: *"Could your travel budget be $100 less for a few months?"*

I recommend starting with the previous options described above first. The final two options below are a last resort.

 Income and paychecks.
Could we change withholding slightly for a couple pay periods, for a little more take-home pay? Can we do 2% less to a 401(k) for a couple pay periods? Is there a plan to take on some extra work for extra cash?

 Student loans.
When folks go back to school, these go on forbearance or deferment. I may say, *"This is an education for you, what if you put one of the loans on deferment for six months?"*

Some of these decisions aren't big-money amounts, but their impact can be scary nonetheless to people who already aren't feeling great about their personal finances. So, it's important to reinforce the benefits of the decisions they're making – even if the amounts don't add up to your full coaching fee:

"We just found $300 based on these short-term actions you're taking, and I'm confident you'll find the other $200. I don't know those ways yet, but I have faith that if you make

even half of those other changes, the other $200 will be there. You're going to have to decide now to take that leap of faith and trust that. Right now, we may have to put it on a credit card – but I fully believe that will be a small impact for a long-term gain. What do you think of that?"

Final Thoughts

If you're still wondering how you should be approaching client sales conversations, let me share a story before we move on, from my own, non-coaching experience.

Michael and I wanted to have our driveway redone. It had developed cracks and holes over the years and had become downright unsightly. We called two contractors for bids. The first person arrived and after I showed him the driveway and explained my concerns, he said, *"What would you like us to do? Do you want us to dig it up and redo it, or patch it, or just lay new concrete over it?"*

He's the expert, right? But here he is, asking me what approach I want to take with this problem. I knew nothing about concrete, so I had no idea what to tell him. I asked him what he thought.

"It's personal preference," he replied with a shrug. He offered an approximate cost and then left.

The second contractor showed up and we looked at the driveway. He said, *"Here's what's going on with your driveway, and here's what caused it."* He described two options in detail, each with a different price and with different outcomes. He said very clearly, *"Your driveway is X, and you want Y. You can achieve that by doing one of two things. One is good, the other is better. Here's what one will provide that the other will not, but either could be an option for you."*

He quoted the prices for both options and asked if I had any questions. He said he'd follow up in a couple of days to see which one we'd decided on.

Which contractor would you hire? For Michael and I, it was a no-brainer. In my interaction with the second contractor, I felt informed, supported, and yes, led through the sales process. Sure enough, he called a few days later and we hired him. The other contractor never bothered to follow up.

Remember, your clients are looking to you to inform, support, and guide them. That's how you gain their trust and earn their business.

Still not sure you can master sales techniques? For practice, I suggest going to a store where you'd be buying a higher-end item – say, electronics, appliances, or furniture – and shop for something. Observe the things you like about the salesperson, and also the things you don't like. What makes this sales encounter a positive experience? What parts give you pause, or even start to counter the positive vibes?

> Remember, your clients are looking to you to inform, support, and guide them.

Most people say they "don't like" sales, but it's an entire process and you'll most likely find there are certain facets of it that you enjoy and appreciate. It's great, for instance, when a salesperson really listens to you, educates you, and takes the time to find out what you want and why.

To be a successful financial coach, learn to be that type of salesperson!

Chapter 03

Action Summary

- [ ] 1. Reflect on your past experiences in sales conversations.

- [ ] 2. Identify ways you can plant seeds throughout your Discovery Session.

- [ ] 3. Ask yourself why it's in the client's best interest for you to be good at sales conversations - understand this answer intimately.

- [ ] 4. Work through the Sales Objection questions provided.

TREAT
OBJECTIONS
as requests
FOR FURTHER
INFORMATION.

• BRIAN TRACEY •

I've had so many fantastic conversations with clients since going through this session - conversations that wouldn't have otherwise come about. The ability to perceive what's holding a client back and then develop an exercise to identify it, work through it, and then develop a plan to go forward has been helpful in ensuring my clients' success.

NICK ELKINS

FAMILY FINANCE FREEDOM

Chapter 04

Designing Programs & Onboarding Clients

The end of the Discovery Session should trigger a series of email "touches" from you to the client:

1. Return their worksheet with their numbers, notes, etc.

2. A follow-up campaign that consists of three separate email messages:

   A. An action list and summary of the Discovery Session.

   B. A check-in email that includes "before-and-after" statistics of clients who continue with coaching. If you don't have statistics, you could use testimonials or emotional transformations. This message includes a link to schedule their Next Steps consultation if it isn't already scheduled.

   C. A final check-in, one month from the date of the Discovery Session. The message here is, *"By now, you should have accomplished X, Y, and Z. If not, here's what could be holding you back – and we eat these problems for breakfast! So, don't be ashamed to share with us whatever is going on."*

You'll want to craft these email messages to reinforce the good advice you've already provided and to invite the sales conversation by discussing future coaching options. How can the client continue to receive support, coaching, and accountability? What do they need to feel confident and continue on their financial journey?

Again, your clients will look to you to guide them.

Let's say the client is interested in further coaching services at the end of the Discovery Session. However, by now you've come to the end of your session, so there's really no time to delve into the particulars. Now, it's time to schedule the "onboarding" appointment, or what we call the "Welcome Call."

You can say something like, *"Let's get you scheduled for a 30-minute phone call. On that call, we'll go over the steps that need to happen between now and your next appointment. In the meantime, I'm going to send you the contract so you can read through it – and if you have questions, we can talk about them on the call."*

Don't worry that they're leaving the Discovery Session without having already signed an agreement. The people who leave and then change their minds weren't going to be good clients for you anyway – or you'll soon be able to coach them through what might be stopping them. This might be their own fears.

Two critical points here:

 Show your excitement, energy, and confidence in discussing these next steps. When this session ends, the client can't help but think, 'Wow, what have I gotten myself into?' It's understandable – and their positive impression of you and your ability to assist them will make all the difference in keeping them on board. Give them a little pep talk to reinforce their enthusiasm and yours.

 Schedule the onboarding call within one or two days after the Discovery Session, while everything is fresh in their mind and before they've had a chance to start second-guessing themselves: Do I really have the time for this? Do I really want to spend this money?

When you email the contract for future services to them, the welcome call is also really important. This helps get the contract signed and wrap up the onboarding process. **(Before you start using a contract, be sure to have a lawyer review it that is familiar with business laws in your state).**

In my business, someone from my office makes the call: *"I'm calling to let you know what to expect these coming few months. The process can be intense at first, and we want to make sure things go as smoothly as possible. We want to review the agreement with you and answer any questions or concerns you have, so you'll feel confident as we get started."*

There are several steps to walking them through the contract by phone:

☐ Let them hear your excitement and that you're honored that they chose to move forward. We don't take this lightly. We don't take it for granted. They're not "just a client" to us – they're now part of our family, and that's a big deal.

- ☐ Review the agreement, summarize, and ask if they have any questions. We recommend they simply click the buttons and then sign as we go through it, so it's done.

- ☐ Take their credit card information and arrange the next meeting date.

- ☐ Get their future appointments scheduled – as many as they want.

- ☐ Let them know the next steps and what to expect for their first session.

- ☐ Reassure them and, once again, share your excitement that they're on board.

We most often do this by phone, although I sometimes follow it up with a video emailed to them, saying I'm excited and can't wait for their first meeting.

Tips For The Best Client Experience

You are the leader. You are guiding them and leading them through the process. The process is what it is, it's complete because it works, and there's no hesitation and no confusion. You LEAD their process.

You are the expert. You decide which program is best for them based on what they want, and trust that you know what it will take to get them there. You can see their situation better than they can, because they may be overwhelmed by their immediate crisis or other priorities in their lives. You know how to bring it all into focus.

Listen to your client. At the start of every meeting, especially the first few, I ask, *"Tell me what is going well and what you like about this process. Also tell me what isn't going so well and what you don't like so far."* This will allow them to guide the speed at which you coach them initially. You don't want to overwhelm them; the idea is to push them, but not bombard them. It lets them know you're open to feedback and that you want to customize the process for their needs. Finally, it allows you to learn important insights about how they're handling the pressure, and how they handle change overall.

Take a few minutes to reflect on each session. Especially in your early interactions with clients, jot some notes to yourself immediately after the session. What were your impressions? Is there anything you could have done better, or might have said differently? Based on what they said, what might you add to their next session? If you wait until the end of the day or the following day, you'll forget some of these important insights.

Designing Your Coaching Programs

One of the biggest challenges I faced in starting my financial coaching business was designing my coaching programs – crafting the packages of services I would offer and deciding what I would charge for them. This is another area where you can learn from my mistakes, to design your own programs that will be successful.

Any financial planner can sit down with clients for a one-time advice session. The idea behind a financial coaching program is to lead the client through a series of changes. Here are three of the program outlines I attempted and why, in my experience, they didn't work very well:

1. One session per month, or pay-per-session.

- One session per month when a client is learning a whole new way to think, act, and manage their money didn't make sense.

- Pay-by-session doesn't encourage consistency. It also makes every client contact way too reactionary – they reach out when something goes wrong or they're in crisis mode.

- If you think about it, what a client needs early in the coaching process is likely very different than what they need many months or years later. So, trying to use the same pay-per-session system for everyone didn't make sense.

- A lot can go wrong, or they have more questions, at the beginning of their experience with you. I found myself reacting to client calls constantly.

- This method didn't encourage long-term clients. It didn't give them anything to shoot for. They didn't know what was happening from one month to the next, or if they had "graduated" from anything, hit any milestones, or achieved any certain level of completion.

2. Set a monthly fee for anything, unlimited.

- People would reschedule all the time, thinking it didn't matter if they cancelled because, *"Well, I get unlimited sessions…"*

- When I offered this option, it was the only plan I offered, for every client. Some clients took proper advantage of it, but others did not. I realized there should be a separate plan for those who didn't really need unlimited access.

- This option gives everyone the same level of access – to me. I soon realized that my time and expertise is a commodity that some people will gladly pay more for. So, those who truly want and will make good use of unlimited access, should pay more for it.

3. A package of a minimum number of sessions, at a set price per session.

- With no specific end date and no fixed schedule, people would spread their sessions out or never end up using all of them. This required a substantial amount of follow-up to try to get them scheduled.

- This open-ended arrangement takes away their sense of urgency to move forward.

In short, when designing my early coaching programs, I soon learned:

- If you're not having a client session, you're generally not getting paid.

- If your system encourages clients to reach out only when they've hit a wall or are facing a crisis, you're likely to have clients who don't schedule appointments regularly or cancel suddenly, making it almost impossible to plan your calendar, your workflow, and your business budget. You also inadvertently enable them to contact you only when they need help putting out a fire or cleaning up the consequences of a poor financial decision.

- For the same reason, drop-in sessions MUST BE the exception. There are some clients for whom scheduled appointments never seem to work – but make sure you work with no more than one or two of these "free spirits!" Otherwise, your schedule and budget will suffer.

What came from these insights? I decided that I want to work with clients who, after their eye-opening Discovery Session, want to make big changes. So, I don't allow "just one session" or "drop-in sessions" from there, and I'll encourage you to do the same. Unless you think the problem you can help them solve is truly achievable in a one-session solution, just decide now that it isn't an option. I get asked all the time (and you will too), *"Can I schedule with you for a quick follow-up?"*

The answer is NO.

If something isn't working in their financial picture, it's all connected. We're not going to figure out what it is in one session. They must commit to diving into the everyday nuances of their problem, so we can be the experts and solve it. They'll need to keep me updated on their finances in order for us both to see the results. That's more than a one-time conversation.

My philosophy with money is that to truly solve a problem, you have to get close to it, get really involved. So, after the Discovery Session, a client's only option is to let me in completely and partner with me at a FULL COMMITMENT level.

We lay an amazing, solid, clear foundation for them, which is intense at first. After that initial phase, I can help them semi-annually. In other words, they have to EARN the right

> ...to truly solve a problem about money, you have to get really close and involved with it.

to graduate to a "cheaper," less involved coaching package. But initially, they've got to be all in. They can't skip the hard work on the front of this process.

I'm stressing this point because newer coaches are often hesitant, even afraid, to require this level of commitment and set high expectations for their clients. Think about it this way – if you haven't got their commitment and you have low expectations for them, what types of clients do you think you'll attract?

Recommending A Program

You will have different programs at different price levels, but I've learned not to offer all of them to a client as options. As their coach, you will almost always know which program they'd get the most benefit from – and remember, they are looking to you to guide them. By spelling out too many options, you'll overwhelm them – and they'll ask you what you think anyway!

So, don't be shy about making a recommendation:

"Based on your budget, your goals, and the overall changes we've talked about you making, I think the best option for you is (name the package or program). In that package, we'll do (list a few of the results they would get, based on the notes you have about this client and what they want)."

The more time I can spend with clients, the more challenges I can give them and the more helpful concepts I can teach them. I've developed a one-month IGNITE program; a four-month GOALS & DREAMS program; and a seven-month TOTAL TRANSFORMATION program. The names have changed a few times, but these are the current coaching options. Each begins with weekly coaching sessions for a month.

The <u>one-month</u> program ends after four sessions. Very few people select this program. The price is the highest, per session – remember, I reward clients who commit for a longer period of time. The first month is also the most labor-intensive for me, getting to know the clients, their financial realities, and attitudes. But in four weeks of coaching, I can get them organized, establish some new systems and habits, and give them plenty of encouragement to launch on their own. This option is really only reserved for individuals experiencing a big life transition, such as a divorce. We create a plan and get them organized, but because of the transition they're experiencing, setting long-term goals is difficult, likely because there are too many unknowns at that time. We offer this option to help them put a solid, interim plan in place and encourage them to come back once the dust settles, when we can really hit the ground running with one of our other options. Otherwise, this option is never even shared with a client who isn't experiencing a transition.

 The <u>four-month</u> program includes one month of weekly coaching sessions, and then a session every other week after that. That's a total of 10 sessions. I get all the same systems set up as in the one-month program, but then challenge the clients' behaviors, within their new budget, to make that budget work for them to meet their goals and dreams. There's a lot more goal-setting work in this program. We look months or a year or two into the future.

 The <u>seven-month</u> program is one month of weekly coaching, then six months of every-other-week sessions. That's a total of 16 sessions. This program focuses on the big picture – a client's entire financial life, guiding principles, and mind-set about money.

When clients have finished a four-month or seven-month program, if we all agree there are still issues to work on, or if new issues have cropped up, we can offer them an additional three-month "re-up" at an additional price.

With each of these packages, because we're meeting with clients so often – weekly or every other week – we find there's very little need for them to contact us between visits, although we make it clear to them that they're always welcome to reach out if they have questions. Occasionally, if someone in a four- or seven-month program is really struggling despite their best efforts, I'll add an extra appointment and not charge them.

Pricing And Payments

My financial coaching services are not inexpensive. However, as I've mentioned before, people value your services at the level you value them – and in my view, we over-deliver for our clients and our service is priceless! I am a priority, based on what I know I can do for stressed-out prospective clients who come to me with serious financial challenges and a sincere interest in improving their entire relationship with money.

> People value your services at the level you value them.

You can charge for your program in one of two ways: pay-in-full or a payment plan. I prefer to mention my prices as a monthly fee since that is how the majority of my clients choose to pay. But I offer a ten percent discount if they want to pay-in-full at the start of the program. Accepting payments requires more effort, follow up, and tracking. So I offer a small bonus by removing that administrative work. Conversely, you can set a price for the full program and tack on ten percent if they want the convenience of making payment. I prefer the first option because I am offering a perk or a discount should they choose to pay-in-full. With the second approach, you are stating the price as a penalty for wanting to make payment. The math may be identical, but the energy behind each approach is not.

In terms of the number of payments, make sure they'll be fully paid up before you finish working with them. For our seven-month program, they can make up to seven payments, and so on.

Have the money conversation up front, early, and consistently. I might mention the price for the "next step" to a client and say, *"Usually, people choose either the 1st or the 15th of the month as payment dates. I can see that this isn't an affordability issue; it's about whether you see the value we can create together for that amount, and where you'll be if you don't do it."*

I don't sit and wait for their reaction. Instead, I ask, *"What kinds of questions do you have about this?"* or *"What kinds of concerns are showing up for you?"* I prefer to have more direct communication with them than wonder what they're thinking.

Later, in a four-month or seven-month program, the client might feel awkward talking with you about what might happen next. They most likely don't know there are other programs they could transition to that cost less and take less time. So, make sure to bring it up yourself: *"We've got three sessions left in this program, and I wanted to make sure you understand your options going forward."* They'll most likely be relieved that you brought it up.

In my coaching practice, clients have to choose the 1st or 15th as due dates for their payments. I have their credit card on file and set them up in my merchant account as automatic. (This eliminates the need for monthly invoicing.) You could use Stripe or Paypal, but Paypal charges for the additional feature of allowing recurring payments and requires you to send an invoice. You want to avoid having to send invoices; it's much less hassle to set up ongoing monthly charges or debits.

> Every minute you spend asking for payment, you're doubting your value.

Setting automatic payments allows me to avoid awkward money conversations. I promise these are never easy or fun for anyone, and can really put us in a funk as coaches and business owners. Every minute you spend asking for payment, you're doubting your value, making it into something bigger than it is, feeling insecure, feeling bad for having to bring it up, and so on. It isn't worth it!

I've chosen not to mention how many sessions the client gets in each of our programs in my scripts, sales conversations, and the marketing flyers we distribute. I've found that, for the most part, the client doesn't really care – they just want to know that I'm going to help them.

One of the most terrifying concepts to a coach who is first starting out is: what do you do if a client gets results faster? Or gets through the work faster than, say, four months? In reality, this is one of the best gifts to a new coach! Out of necessity, you will likely think of another exercise or skill you can teach them. You'll see something else that you can talk with them about. It may be another financial challenge they're also experiencing – something you couldn't even think about or focus on until the initial problem was solved – and you'll be able to add MORE value for them. Once you do that often enough, you can actually create a whole new program – perhaps a graduate-level type of program – so you can continue working with clients even longer. You'll learn more about this option in Chapter 8.

Now that you know what goes into creating my financial coaching programs – try designing one of your own!

Below, the *Design Your Client Programs* exercise will help you create the content and information necessary for your client coaching programs.

Design Your Client Programs

What SUP2ER Problem are you solving?

What steps can you take to help them work through the problem?

What skills does the client need to learn to solve the above problem?

What steps can you take to help them learn these skills?

What exercises can you have the client complete that will help them?

What goals do you have for the client?

How many meetings (on average) will it take to complete the steps, exercises, and skill-setting you outlined above?

How long will it take (on average) for the client to work through the steps, exercises and skill-setting you listed above?

Focusing on what the client GAINS from this program, what is a good name for it?

Based on all of the above details, what is the price of this program?

What payment options are there for this program?

What maintenance or reinforcement may be needed as the client works through this problem?

After the client solves this problem, does a new problem arise? (If so, begin from the top and work your way through these questions again to design the next program.)

You'll be developing different programs at different price levels, but for now, start by creating a program around the number one problem – the SUP2ER problem – you think you'll be helping people solve through your coaching. Come up with fun and appropriate names for your programs, while trying to make it obvious to the client what they can expect.

Characteristics Of A Program

1. A set length of time and fixed number of scheduled appointments.

2. How long will it take you to solve the problem you're setting out to solve?

3. Based on the results you want them to achieve, how often do you think you'll need to be meeting? (The number of sessions will be determined by answering this.)

4. What and how much maintenance and reinforcement will be needed along the way as they work through this problem? (This is why I offer the three-month "re-up.")

5. Can you reward them for the benefits you'd like to encourage? (Positive reinforcement is key. If there's a particular "milestone" they've achieved, is there something you could do to recognize them for it? Send a card, maybe a book in the mail, announce it as a great example to others? Don't wait until the end result is achieved to reward progress!)

6. Does the program include email support?

7. Do they get cell phone access to you? (Not recommended if you want any semblance of work/life balance!)

A final note: Once your programs are in place, don't feel you have to make big changes based on one client's experience. If someone gets through your seven-month program in six months, don't stress and start rethinking the whole program. Focus instead on trends that fit the majority of your clients. There will always be some exceptions, but keep the averages in mind when designing your programs.

Creating Content That Gets Clients Results

Creating content helps you demonstrate the skills you want clients to learn.

By "content," I'm not talking about marketing. I'm talking about what a client needs to know and creating a concept, process, and/or worksheet that clearly illustrates each point.

This is one of my personal favorite parts of financial coaching. At a seminar, I was once asked, *"If you could spend only four hours a week on your business, how would you spend that time?"* For me, hands down, it is creating content – figuring out how to teach financial skills in ways that are practical, easy to follow, inspiring, and that cut out a lot of the clutter that people don't really need to know.

This field is so vast and so important that there's plenty of content I haven't even thought of yet! So, please don't limit your own coaching to the concepts that I already use and will be sharing with you in this playbook. You'll find there's plenty of room for you to be creative and come up with your own content as well.

I think when I got good at creating content is when I let go of the idea that there's one way everyone should manage their money. I got better at content creation when I started to explore and question things, asking 'why' instead of accepting every financial tip or budgeting method I ran across.

One of the biggest fallacies in the world is that managing money is common sense.

What we educate people about is not always profound to us as coaches. For example, let's take the concept of net worth. I've known what net worth was since college. But I can't tell you how many clients either have no idea what this is or how it is determined; or they don't understand why they should care about it. If you can help them relate to that concept in a whole new way, or put a unique spin on it – that's the power of coaching.

Stop thinking about the knowledge you have as common sense. One of the biggest fallacies in the world is that managing money is common sense. This is why so many people struggle with it – because they're "supposed to be good at it."

This also will help allay your fears as you build your coaching business – those nagging doubts that, since financial prowess is "common sense," why would anyone need your help figuring it out? You need to trust that you have enough knowledge, right this minute, to help someone else.

One good exercise for content creation is to take a basic financial concept that you've known for so long, you don't even remember where or when you first learned it. Try to break down exactly what you know and why you know it! Perhaps trace the steps you followed to understand it better or figure out how it relates to you. Breaking it down into steps helps you discover how to teach this concept to others.

Take any financial topic – interest rates, behavioral spending, student-loan debt, budgeting, calculating savings rates – and adopt this perspective as a financial coach:

- *How can I demonstrate this concept in a way that will make sense to the client? Start general, then get more specific or customized.*

- *What would make sense to me? Not now, based on all my current knowledge, but when I didn't know all that I know now. If I were just learning this concept for the first time, what would I need to know?*

- *How can I make this VISUAL to the client?*

- *How can I take this knowledge a step further than what's out there?*

- *What does my client ultimately care about, and how can I make this relevant?*

Assume that everything you know is fresh and unique to the client in front of you. Of course, some exercises will be profound for one person – and just 'so-so' for another. Don't expect an eye-opening, revolutionary impact every time. But even for folks who are naturally gifted with money, there is always – always – more they can learn about financial management, goal setting, and so on. It's good for you, as a coach, to take note of what topics pique the most interest or get people excited or inspired.

On the next page, brainstorm a list of skills or topics around which you'd like to create a handout or exercise. Make another list of skills or topics you'd like to learn more about. Get organized!

I'd Like To Create A Handout For...

. . . .

I'd Like To Learn More About...

. . . .

> "When we are in the process of creating something, we must have flexibility of mind to move with what needs to be done. What allows this to happen is precisely the fact that we're not attached to how things should be done."
>
> - JOSEPH JAWORSKI,
> AUTHOR AND LEADERSHIP DEVELOPMENT EXPERT

Creating Content That Matters

I create content through curiosity and exploration. That might sound more like a slogan than a piece of advice, but it is absolutely true. Here are the steps I typically take:

1. I observe a need in my clients. For example, SELF-RELIANCE; I'm noticing that some of my clients demonstrate sincere and natural self-reliance and others not so much. That thought intrigues me. Another example is CONFORMING – I wonder, why do some people need to conform to social norms, while others are just as determined to ignore them? How does each attitude affect their personal finances?

2. I started using Todoist (list and task management software) to organize these ideas, but you can organize them anywhere – Pinterest or Asana (work management software), in a notebook, etc. – whatever works for you. I have a project entitled "Topics to Discover," and I add to that list as new topics occur to me.

3. Once I begin researching a topic, I'll create a separate project for it. I have one entitled "Self-Reliance" and another called "Conforming," for example. Some topics will take weeks to fully digest; others will come together within a couple of days.

4. Now, I begin digesting information. I'll search online for "podcast about self-reliance" or "psychology behind self-reliance" or "ways to become more self-reliant." Sure, not everything you'll find will relate to your clients, or even to personal finance – but you can come up with some great material just by casting a wide net. What you may also find is that some topics really don't pan out once you start digging deeper, and that's okay, too.

5. I think, 'What does my client need to know about this?' That helps me create an educational component – as a Microsoft Word document or on Google Drive – in which I summarize what I've learned, mention the most interesting parts, etc. I also paste the links to the original material so I can find it again – and in some cases, pass these resources along to clients.

6. I create an action-oriented task list: Things to ponder or questions to ask yourself. (You can use these questions to spark conversation in your client meetings.) Actions to take. Steps to follow. Changes I want to make. How to use this info to get them to commit – to a dollar amount, an energy level, a schedule. With this step, you're figuring out how to make the new knowledge relevant. What steps can the client take to gain an awareness of how this concept applies to them or their life?

7. Consider the commitment level and how to achieve buy-in. Now that the client knows more about this topic (education) and why it's relevant to them (action), what do they want to do about it? It might be setting a goal, committing to a particular mindset, or taking a daily or weekly action.

8. Pull it together in a handout or create a document in Canva, the do-it-yourself design website. This is the visual component of the coaching process. Just talking about some of these concepts isn't good enough. You'll need to reinforce the lesson with some visual components and exercises.

Frankly, the visual aspect of content creation is not so fun for me, and I mention this because it's okay to recognize that there are some parts of this process that you'll enjoy more than others. In my case, I hand my research over to Michael, who enjoys the visual design elements. I explain what I want, sometimes sketch it out on a scratch piece of paper, and finalize it as needed after he's created a draft. You might also have someone you can collaborate with. It's a good strategy to have more than one set of eyes on the documents.

Does your handout make the point? Does it have the desired impact? Then it's good enough! It's probably not the best use of your time as a coach to make sure everything you design is a work of art.

Online Sources For Creating Content

How do you create your content, branding, or other marketing materials when that type of skill isn't in what you think of as your "zone of competence?" We suggest the gig economy, with sites like Fiverr, where you can hire freelance talent to design a logo or a website, edit video – just about anything you would need. Prices can be as low as $5 and all the way up to hundreds of dollars, depending on the level and amount of work needed. Fiverr is a great place to start when you want branding or marketing material created quickly and for less money than hiring a graphic designer or branding specialist to do a complete job for you.

Strikingly.com and Wix.com are places where you can create a website. Their prices are reasonable and the design function is very user friendly. All you have to do is "drag and drop" to create a very nice website. In my experience, they are much easier to use than a website like Wordpress.com, for example, where you need to have some knowledge of HTML coding to create an effective website.

If you are okay with using HTML coding and creating your own website that way, Siteground.com is a great site host. We have found their customer service is excellent and is included in the hosting price.

We recommend Google Suites online softwares for your computer. You can create documents, slides, spreadsheets, and forms (like feedback surveys), and you can easily share them online.

We create tutorials and email videos in Loom. It allows you to put your face on the screen while sharing other data on-screen at the same time. Another option for this is Screencast-o-matic.

A Few More Online Sources For Content Creation

1. **Savvy Spreadsheets (savvyspreadsheets.com):** This website calls itself "your source for user-friendly, downloadable Excel templates."

2. **Canva (canva.com):** The tagline here is, "Design Anything. Publish Anywhere." It has an extensive free-use photo library, tons of templates for everything from business cards to flyers, and more.

3. **Microsoft Word:** Word offers users hundreds of templates to choose from for flyers, worksheets, posters, and so on.

4. **Apple Pages (apple.com/pages):** This is a handy design tool for Mac users.

5. **Microsoft PowerPoint:** Another Microsoft product, PowerPoint offers dozens of templates for creating slides to accompany your presentations to clients or business groups.

6. **Loom (loom.com):** As mentioned above, as a website or app, Loom allows you to record audio or video and share it with others. Their website (useloom.com/use-cases) highlights case studies of several ways to use the service.

7. **Vertex42 (vertex42.com):** The folks behind this site are masters with Excel. I love the variety of spreadsheets available and the customization that's been added to them. They provide a personal use download. If you're going to use it for your business with your clients, check out the commercial use license, which is very reasonably priced and ensures that you're respecting their intellectual property.

8. **Google Drive:** You can use a free version of Google Doc, Sheets, Slides as well and access them from your cloud account on Google Drive.

Apps, software, and online programs are ever-changing, with new options added constantly. For updated recommendations, check out the Financial Coach Academy blog, where we often chat about things we've tried. It's financialcoachacademy.com.

The learning curve might be a little steep for people who aren't techies, but you will soon find that many of the recommended sites are easy to use. You might even discover that creating your own unique content can be a lot of fun!

Chapter 04

Action Summary

☐ **1. Design a program offering for your clients:**

    a. Outline the skills you will want to teach them and the amount of time required to teach these skills.

    b. Set price and payment options.

    c. Determine the best meeting schedule and timeline.

    d. Consider all the characteristics required for your program.

☐ **2. Create organizational structure:**

    a. Create a system for managing ideas as they come to you.

    b. Develop a way to organize thoughts and research more in-depth topics.

☐ **3. Begin creating exercises to facilitate your clients' learning.**

COMING
TOGETHER
IS A
beginning.

KEEPING
TOGETHER IS
progress

WORKING
TOGETHER IS
success.

• HENRY FORD •

I began my financial coaching business using social media to gain clients. I never thought of using referral partners who are already in front of my ideal client to help me build my business. I didn't have a lot of confidence in how to present my services to them. Through the marketing lesson, I really felt confident enough to reach out to potential referral partners! If it wasn't for the Financial Coach Academy, I wouldn't have thought to do this or had the confidence to do it!

MANDYY THOMAS

MANDYY THOMAS COACHING

Chapter 05

Marketing Your Services

The truth is, no one really wants to market their products or services. It takes time. It often costs money, since it can involve steps like placing ads. It can feel awkward when you're cold-calling or striking up conversations; and of course, there's the fear of rejection, particularly if you're somewhat introverted. It's hard to know where to start and what will work.

But not marketing? That's like saying, *"No, I don't want a paycheck!"*

In the more than a decade that our financial coaching practice has been in business, we've tried all sorts of marketing techniques and strategies. In this chapter, you'll learn about those that have worked well along the way – and those that have not. Please note that even though some of the strategies didn't work for us, they might actually work for you.

The first paradigm shift that I encourage you to make is to try not to think of marketing as sales, because it's really so much more. It encompasses every facet of the public "face" of your business, from your email signature and business cards, to your social media presence, your processes for connecting with clients, and even how you handle errors when they occur.

When first starting out, we have found that you'll need to spend about 5 hours per week on marketing. Once your business is set up, you might find that much of this time will be spent talking and listening to referral partners and clients one-on-one. In financial coaching, it's the conversations that seal the deal.

You don't have to be extroverted to be engaging. If you tend to be an introvert, try reading books and articles to help bolster your confidence. The book *How to Win Friends and Influence People* by Dale Carnegie – first published in the 1930s – remains one of the best, and is still widely available. Heck, there's even a Wikipedia page that summarizes its major takeaways!

Introverts should also consider reading *Quiet: The Power of Introverts in a World That Can't Stop Talking* by Sarah Cain to dispel the myth that society finds extroversion ideal and introversion inferior. She says that introverts have their own strengths and benefits and that they should be effectively harnessed and utilized in a society that is built for extroverts.

There's no good time to start marketing. But you want a paycheck, right? So, just wade in and start, using the tips in this chapter.

Pearls Of Marketing Wisdom

You might have heard this old one-liner: Do you know what they call the person who finished dead last in their class at medical school?

Doctor.

Yes, folks go to doctors all the time without knowing how 'good' or 'bad' they are. It is clear, however, that the good doctors are those who are personable, have great bedside manner, and actually care about their patients as people, in addition to knowing their stuff.

The point is, we're not selling expertise, we're selling relationships. Our expertise is assumed by the social proof or credibility we provide in the overall marketplace. The better your website is, the better and more interesting your social media posts look, the more people you're meeting, the more presentations you give or TV interviews you do, the more solid your social proof becomes.

The SUP2ER Problems you defined in Chapter 1 will help you focus your marketing messages, just as they help you understand who your ideal clients are and what you want to help them with. Remember, these are personal finance concerns or issues that are **S**pecific to the client, **U**rgent, **P**ersistent, **P**ervasive, **E**xpensive, and **R**ecognizable.

Think about most of the ads you see or hear in a day. Most don't scream, *"Attention all women, ages 25 to 50!"* Instead, whether it's with humor, or nostalgia, or caring, they show how to solve a problem for a person who, most often, happens to be in a specific age group. The actors in the ad, the language, the setting – all are geared toward a particular demographic. But the point of the ad is SOLVING THE PROBLEM. If you propose to solve the problem, the ad will resonate with those people who need the problem solved.

In revamping their financial life, your client faces a choice: Having you perform the service or doing it themselves. Seen through that lens, your biggest competitors are actually your prospective clients. So, don't allow them to leave you without addressing their comments and concerns. I suggest not asking if they have questions, but rather, what their concerns are. Why? Because questions don't stop people from moving forward. But concerns most definitely stop people from moving forward.

> Your biggest competitors
> are actually your
> prospective clients.

Don't use fear-based marketing. Instead, use marketing to alleviate people's fears. One example is car buying, which typically involves sales tactics that prompt (or some would say 'force') people to make an emotional decision. Car salespeople get a bad rap, but think about it this way: If they relied on customers' rational, logical thought processes, most customers would leave the car lot, think about it for 24 hours or so, and then make their decision – and there's a much higher probability that decision would be 'no.'

In financial coaching, if the client tends to be a strictly rational, logical type of person, you might challenge them to consider their emotional side, and vice versa. The message here is simple: Before you try to satisfy "the client" (or customer), do your best to understand and satisfy the person.

Marketing for financial coaching has some similarities to marriage counseling. A lot of people need it, and even know they need it, but are afraid to take action. There's a lot of denial when people are in a personal financial crisis, and there also are folks who either don't know or choose to ignore how bad their situation is.

If you needed a marriage counselor, would you hire someone you saw in an ad, or on Facebook? No, you're probably more likely to get the advice of a close friend, a doctor, or therapist. So, while maintaining a presence in ads and social media is important, you're not doing it so much to drive business. You're doing it to build name recognition and support growing your network of direct referrals. That's why it is critical to come from a place of authenticity and integrity with your marketing, just as you would with everything you do.

Always view your marketing efforts as supplemental to having good, consistent conversations – never as a replacement for them.

What Are You Good At?

Answer these questions:

What do you think FedEx is good at?

What do you think Disneyland is good at?

What do you think Lexus is good at?

And finally…what are YOU good at, as a financial coach?

You might say FedEx is good at delivering packages overnight; Disneyland is good at rides and family entertainment; and Lexus is good at making high-end vehicles. But I would argue that FedEx is actually good at logistics; Disneyland is good at creating a detailed, magical, and memorable family experiences; and Lexus is good at creating a luxury experience.

As a financial coach, what I feel I am good at is:

 Taking the stress out of money

 Making the stuffy, boring topic of money fun and manageable

 Thinking 'outside the box' about how people think, feel, and communicate about money

 Turning complex topics, like personal finance, into steps that are simple and easy to follow

What would your answer be? And does it reflect the bigger picture, not just specific, individual skills? Your prospective clients don't want to buy a budget or a debt payoff strategy, and they don't want to buy your process. They want to talk with someone who'll listen to them and show them ways to feel better about their financial picture. They're looking for solutions to their most pressing financial challenges.

What did you say you were good at? With all this in mind, would you change your answer?

Conversations Create Cash

At Fiscal Fitness, our theory is, "conversations create cash." Think about a time when you were totally uninterested in a product, a movie, a band – until you talked with one or two people who told you they're great and you HAVE to check them out. For me it was *Downton Abbey*. I saw commercials and read articles about how good it was, but I didn't actually watch it until I finally heard how out-of-this-world-good it was from enough friends and family. No matter how many ads you've seen for a movie until someone you know or trust recommends it, you're a lot less likely to make the time to see it. It's the "know-like-trust" factor. To buy something from someone, we have to feel these things.

Here's another maxim: "Gold bars, not gold stars." The "gold stars" are marketing activities we think we're supposed to do, or milestones we assume we're supposed to meet. We usually pay a lot of money for these, and they might look terrific – but they don't actually get us more clients. From the custom-designed logo to the fancy website, we convince ourselves we're supposed to have them because "everybody else" does, but the high cost means it'll take a lot of new clients in order to pay for these extras.

Gold stars also have a sneaky way of holding you back, especially when you're first establishing your business. You feel you CANNOT start working with clients until you have this, this, and this, all lined up and perfect. You need to check everything off your list before you're really "ready."

This is nonsense! We believe in messy action. Get going!

On the other hand, "gold bars" are the high return-on-investment (ROI) marketing activities. They work for you, have high conversion rates, and build your expertise organically.

You can work on your logo or your website endlessly. But it's having conversations that will result in committed clients. One of the 2017 graduates of the Financial Coach Academy has a full client load, despite having no logo and no website!

Participating in networking groups is a "gold bar" activity. Think about opportunities that not only get you in front of prospective clients, but in front of people who know prospective clients. I'll talk more about referral partners later in the chapter. In the meantime, remember that harnessing the power of networking groups is one of the best ways to build a list of "power referral partners."

Pyramid Of Bankruptcy

How we *think* we should spend money to grow our business.

Pyramid Of Growth

How we should *actually* spend money to grow our business.

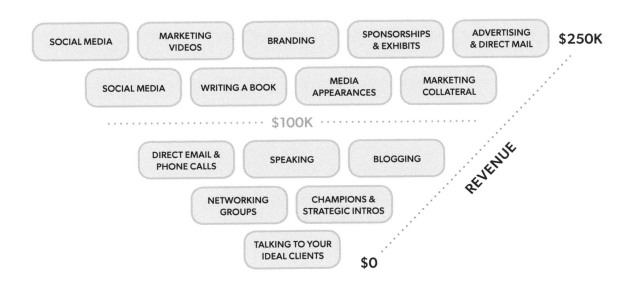

> ... having conversations will result in committed clients.

Where to network? Business Network International (BNI) is a business networking group with chapters in many major cities. Membership costs several hundred dollars a year. It is also very structured and can require a lot of work, including continuously giving referrals to other members and scheduling one-on-one meet-ups to learn more about them.

BNI is actually how I got started getting clients. In my first year of financial coaching full time I joined a local BNI chapter. Following the BNI structure and philosophy over the first year of membership helped me completely fill my client load. After a few more years of membership, I was too busy working with clients to be able to participate fully so I gave up my membership. The relationships I made during that time continue to provide steady referrals today.

There are plenty of less expensive options: Rotary Club, Kiwanis, and Toastmasters all come to mind. Chambers of Commerce and local business journals sponsor meet-up events as well. Small business development centers or business incubators often associated with universities have events. Many cities have small business associations, sales "leads groups," or women's business groups.

Some organizations allow only one member from each profession – one mortgage broker, one pest-control service, one mechanic, etc. That works to your advantage, as there are very few financial coaches. The important thing is to visit as many of these groups as possible and see which ones are a fit for you. Have conversations with the members who could be your potential "power partners" for referrals, and join the organizations you think will be most useful. For financial coaches, look for groups with the types of members who might be interacting with your ideal clients. This could be accountants, bookkeepers, financial advisors, attorneys, realtors, insurance agents, social workers, therapists, debt-relief and credit-repair professionals, and so on.

Here is a basic networking group strategy that works best with BNI, but still could be used with other groups. It really comes down to focus and doing a little bit of homework before you go. BNI allows you to visit a chapter (usually up to two different times) to get a feel for the group and see if it is a right fit for you. They also have every member in every chapter listed along with their profession and business name.

Before you choose to visit a chapter, research the chapters near you (bni.com/find-a-chapter). Look at all of the members of the different chapters and see how many of them are your ideal referral partners. Make a note of their names and their faces if they have a profile photo.

Once you have found 2-3 chapters that seem to have a high number of potential referral partners, schedule a visit. Usually the only cost to visit is the cost of a meal or a cover charge if you don't want to eat.

When you visit, make a bee-line to create conversations with only those members who are your ideal referral partners. Ask questions about their business and share insight about the problems you solve for your ideal clients and then propose a one-to-one meeting at a different time. If you're unable to connect with a member that has a potential to be a referral partner, reach out to them as soon as possible after the meeting to apologize for not being able to chat and inviting them to a one-to-one meeting.

Your end goal for all networking groups is to have a one-on-one with a member that you feel is an ideal referral partner. Whether you are visiting a very structured and transparent group like BNI or maybe going to a Chamber of Commerce meeting, the outcome should be the same. Sometimes it's just that the structure of the meeting isn't conducive to getting in front of that ideal referral partner easily.

12 Business Networking Groups To Maximize Power Partners

- Business Networking International (BNI)
- Area Chambers of Commerce
- Convention & Visitors' Bureau
- Merchant/Professionals groups
- Kiwanis Club
- Meetup
- Mastermind groups
- LeTip
- Local ChooseFi chapter
- Rotary Club
- Optimist Club
- Toastmasters

Referrals From Clients

It's a great feeling when clients send you referrals; it's great to have ambassadors. At the same time, individuals who don't own a business don't understand how to refer properly. Instead they'll say, *"Hey, I referred you to my mom! She totally needs your help."*

They haven't thought about whether Mom is a good fit for me. Is she ready to be coached? We use Excel extensively in our coaching and budgeting process. What if Mom doesn't use the computer for anything but Facebook, and doesn't want to change that? And most importantly, can I solve her SUP2ER Problem?

The other thing clients tend not to do is communicate the best way to reach out to me. They don't think to give people the business line number or my email address, as a businessperson would do with a referral. Instead, I get a Facebook message or a late-night text: *"So-and-so is a client of yours and gave me your name."* (This is one important reason not to give out your cell phone number!)

Coming in this way, outside our system and our normal onboarding process, there's a chance these referrals will get lost in the shuffle.

There are subtle ways to train clients to make referrals properly. Say to the client, *"Here's who I know I can help."* Or even better, *"Here are the problems I eat for breakfast every day!"* Don't focus on people you can't help; mention the characteristics of the person for whom you know you can get results. Or say, *"If you know someone who could use my help, here's the best way to tell them about me. Here's the best way to refer me. Send them to my website. Have them call my office."*

In other words, we have the systems in place because they work. Don't be afraid to educate your clients about what works – and what doesn't.

Do not talk about your clients with their friends or family, or vice versa. They'll ask, *"How did it go? Didn't you love them? What did you say?"* I say, *"It went great. I hope they tell you all about it!"* It is not my place to share this information.

By the same token, when the client who's been referred comes to meet with me, I make sure to tell them in our initial pleasantries, *"I know you were referred by _____. I want you to know that nothing that happens here today will be shared with them. If you want to tell them about it, that's great – but please know that, even if they ask, this conversation is between us, so you never have to worry about that."*

I can sometimes even see a physical change in a client when I say that. People are already feeling nervous about discussing their financial lives, and whether they've considered it or not, the thought that maybe the friends or relatives who referred them would also be privy to the details is an added source of stress or embarrassment.

Never violate that trust. Even in a challenging session, when you have to make observations that the client is not happy to hear or pushes back on, do not ever call the other person who referred you and share this information. If they ask about a referral that isn't going smoothly – and you can tell they know a little bit about what's happening – you can say, *"You can trust that I'm taking good care of the people you refer to me. The conversations we have aren't always easy, but I want you to know that you can trust me."*

You can create a referral program. We've offered two movie passes to anyone who refers a client, for instance. When you're first starting out, a consistent thank-you gift makes sense – you can budget for it and know that it encourages people to refer others to you. Now that I've been in business for a while, I always send a thank-you note, but I send gifts in a more organic fashion. If someone has referred multiple other clients, I might do something special for them.

If you're going to ask for referrals, make sure to train your clients about how to make those referrals.

Referral Partners

If word-of-mouth from current clients is the best resource for connecting with new clients, networking with referral partners is a close second. As part of my marketing time, I set aside 30 minutes a week for having one-on-one conversations with potential referral partners.

Referral partners have skills that complement mine, and some have become great professional friends over time. I can ask their advice – not about specific clients, but about situations – and get a different perspective that makes my coaching better.

Ask yourself, 'Who is in front of my potential clients regularly?' For me, that answer is financial advisors, but also marriage counselors, business coaches, mortgage lenders, realtors. In your area, where are these people? What are the best ways to connect with them? Do you know anyone who could introduce you? And before you meet them, think about the benefits you can offer for them. Why would they refer their clients to you?

> Who is in front of my potential clients regularly?

When you're first starting out, talk with as many people as possible. Set a goal of making a certain number of contacts every week. It's great practice! Explain what you do, share your "Why Story." Sometimes you'll say the wrong things or the right things in the wrong way! That's how you learn. Stop in and introduce yourself at the local financial advisors' offices. Ask family, friends, and clients for introductions to their financial advisors or accountants.

LinkedIn has become a powerful source of scheduling one-on-ones with potential referral partners. In LinkedIn, you can search for specific job titles in specific locations. That means that you can search for "Financial Advisor" in Kalamazoo, MI, and find 985 results. That's 985 potential referral partners that you can message and hopefully schedule a one-on-one.

Don't feel bad when you send out a bunch of messages and don't hear back. Some people don't use LinkedIn who still maintain a profile and some people still don't trust conversations over the internet. We have around a 33% success rate with scheduling one-on-ones with LinkedIn.

Actively reach out to potential referral partners in multiple ways. It might take a dozen points of contact before a person knows, likes, and trusts you, so don't be surprised or assume the worst if it takes multiple touches to get their attention. The ultimate goal is to meet with this person one-on-one, whether it's out for coffee, at their office, or by video chat.

In short, don't just hope and passively send out feelers. Get organized, do your homework, and show some determination, and you will most often be rewarded with attention. In the rare case that doesn't happen, it's probably a sign that the prospective referral just isn't the right fit.

I've created a worksheet to help you identify your ideal referral partners and prepare for a meeting with them. You can find it at **https://www.financialcoachacademy.com/ idealreferralpartner.**

Make A Video!

One super effective way to make an impression during your first contact with potential referral partners is to make a short video using software like Loom (useloom.com). Be personable, and pretend that you're talking right to them.

RESEARCH INDICATES THAT VIDEO EMAILS ARE PROVEN TO HAVE AN 87 PERCENT INCREASE IN "OPENS" AND ENGAGEMENTS.

Do people really open videos from folks they don't know? They will if you make it as appealing as possible!

What a potential referral partner needs to know:

- Your purpose + mission + vision + your "Why Story." Condense content into a 2 minute script.

- The specific types of problems you will help their clients solve.

- Why it's a win/win for them.

End the video with a friendly request for a follow-up phone call.

Financial Advisors As Referral Partners

You might assume that financial advisors would be competitors, and in some cases that is true – those who are fee-based can take the time to work with individuals on budgeting, saving, and debt reduction. But many financial advisors work on commission, and their primary job is to plan for their clients' long-term financial needs. Most do this by selling investments, retirement plans, and insurance products. They don't have the time to dive into someone's entire financial picture like you will as a financial coach, and they're often glad to have you to offer as a referral, to delegate what they don't really do or don't want to do.

When you meet with a financial advisor to discuss your coaching services, do your homework. Look at their website and LinkedIn profile. Who is their target client? You need to know how YOU will be providing value to that client. Even if the advisor focuses on high net-worth clients, you could help the people who those clients find themselves helping or loaning money to consistently – adult children or grandchildren – which indirectly helps the client.

<table>
<tr><td>

Who
is their
target
client?

</td><td>

Focus on making this relationship mutually beneficial. Make it clear that the goal is collaboration, and explain how your services complement theirs: *"My focus is on my client's short-term financial picture and getting them in control of it so that you can help them heading into the future."* And train them so they know how to talk about you and your services. You don't want them to say, *'Oh, you need budgeting help. You need to talk to Kelsa.'*

</td></tr>
</table>

I suggest they say, *"She helps people with more of the day-to-day money concerns. I'm for more long-term focus."*

When you are building a referral partner network you must maintain integrity and authenticity. Be prepared to talk with the financial advisor you are meeting with about how your referral partnerships work. It inevitably comes up in conversation with a new potential referral partner and they want to know how you are going to be referring them new clients.

This is where you have to be open and honest, but also discuss the value of their clients working with you. I relate to them that while I have multiple financial advisors that are referral partners and that the likelihood of us referring them a new client is low, we do make the clients they refer to us better clients for them. Because I can help them improve their day-to-day finances, they are able to invest more and put more money towards their goals. More money invested by their clients means more revenue for them. When I do have a client to refer to a financial advisor, we can pick and choose for the best fit based on location, investment philosophy, ideal clients, etc.

It is important that they know how you want them to refer you, through the website or by giving the client a business card, or even if the financial advisor wants to introduce you, one-on-one or by phone. I feel that puts the client on the spot a little bit. I'd much rather they have time to think about it.

Talk with the advisor about their investment philosophy, so you'll have an idea of what types of clients they have. Ask them financial questions – that way, you'll not only get a bit of training from the advisor, you'll also hear how they explain things and whether they're as clear and effective as they could be.

Eventually, you'll be busy, and you'll want to qualify your referral partners just like you qualify your clients. You'll want to be sure the financial advisors are doing good work – and of course, one way you'll be able to tell is when you see what they've recommended as investment or insurance products to their clients.

When a client tells me, *"I asked my financial advisor about that and she said it's too complicated and not to worry about it,"* that's a red flag. Nothing should be too complicated to explain when you're working with someone's personal finances. It isn't always intentional; financial advisors are busy people, and the question might have come up at the very end of a meeting. But I do notice how my clients talk about the professionals who referred them to me. And if a client comes to me not by referral, I always ask whether they have a financial advisor. If they do, I ask for an email introduction to that advisor.

You also want referral partners to whom you can make referrals. I want to be able to tell a financial advisor, *"I've got these folks' finances in great shape now, and they're ready to talk with a financial advisor about retirement plans! I'd like to send them your way."*

On the other hand, if an advisor refers a client to me, I always send them back to that advisor – and I make sure the advisor knows I'll send them back as a better client, a better steward of their money. If I have concerns about the financial advisor, I make sure to coach the client about how to get more out of that relationship: *"Have you shared your concerns with your advisor? I think that's something they might want to hear."* I might also offer to get the financial advisor on the phone for a three-way conversation, to help bridge the gap if needed.

I do ask clients to sign a confidentiality agreement that says I won't discuss their financial situation with anyone – not even their financial advisor – without their specific written permission. Most people happily sign it. With their permission, they allow me to not only discuss what I'm doing to work with the client, their concerns, and what we're hoping to achieve, but to also ask questions of the financial advisor: *"What challenges do you see them having? What are your observations in your meetings with them?"* This is invaluable information.

After meeting one-on-one with a financial advisor, I make sure to send a thank-you note along with some business cards and flyers in case they have folks who might be referrals. For those who don't need the printed materials, I make a short, personalized video and email it to them, thanking them for their time.

Sometimes, you will find that a financial advisor contacts you directly to explain their services and prospect for clients. In these cases, vet them carefully. We ask them, *"What challenges do you see your clients facing with money that you feel are outside your skill set to help them with?"* If they say, "Nothing," or they don't really know how to answer, they don't really need our help. They want us to refer business to them – but their clients don't need our help.

Building Credibility

Being seen as a go-to source for journalists about financial fitness topics is an excellent way to gain credibility.

Make contact by phone or send a short news release to:

 Local reporters who cover business/consumer topics

 Local editors on assignment at newspapers, TV stations, and magazines

 Local TV and radio show producers and/or talk shows

 Local college radio station and/or student newspaper

Let them know you're available for interviews. If there's a "news hook" – a reason for news coverage – even better: April is Financial Literacy Month. September is National College Savings Month. People always want tips for pre-holiday budgeting or wedding budgets, and so on. Even being a financial coach is a great discussion topic! Offer yourself as a guest on local radio or TV talk shows, or podcasts.

You'll have better luck with this when you do some homework and send to the people who actually cover the topics you want to discuss, or those who make the decisions about what they'll be putting on the air. Watch or listen to the shows you want to target for story pitches; familiarize yourself with their format and personalities. Check out the station's website, and the reporters' and producers' LinkedIn profiles.

Consider signing up for HARO – Help A Reporter Out. An online service of Cision, which calls itself a "global media intelligence company," HARO is a clearinghouse for journalists who need to find people to interview about a wide variety of topics. About three times a day, you'll get email messages letting you know that someone's looking for interviews on a particular topic. If it doesn't relate to you or you can't fit it in, fine – just delete it. But sometimes, it'll result in an interview and your name and quotes in a newspaper article. The service is free to you.

I do not suggest creating and sending out a newsletter unless you have the time to devote to it and to not send it any more frequently than monthly. At Fiscal Fitness Phoenix, we use our newsletter to compile each month's activities, a kind of upbeat recap. We might mention where I've been quoted in news stories, with links to them, and share our favorite blog posts or social media posts, also with links. Rather than long articles, we focus on bite-sized bits of info. And we have a 47 percent open rate for our newsletter emails, as opposed to under 20 percent when it was a long article in one email.

Lead Magnets

You can gain people in your marketing funnel by offering a "freemium" or a "lead magnet." This could be a free worksheet to help organize their debt payoff, a simple budget template, or a video explaining the best way to budget for the holidays. Use an email marketing software, like MailChimp (mailchimp.com), to create a signup form that goes on your website for people to receive your freemium. In return for getting your freemium you get their contact information.

Email campaigns or lead magnets or drip campaigns – what to do depends on who you are and who you're trying to reach. Think about what you've signed up for already and what really catches your eye. There are many free resources out there for how to design them. Just make sure it acts as a sales funnel that drives people to your website, where they can learn more.

 You can make a no-risk offer...or a low-risk offer (giving something away free), which requires the user to give an email address. Statistically, 75 percent of the people who come to your website are simply seeking information. Another 23 percent are comparing your services or products to others, and only 2 percent are actually ready to take action. You have to find ways to nurture them from one point to the other.

Content Marketing Sales Funnel

KNOW

NO-RISK OFFER
(No registration required)

- Blog articles
- Videos
- Podcasts
- Interviews
- Audio files

LOW-RISK OFFER
(Register through email)

- E-books
- Templates
- Reports
- Whitepapers
- Guides
- Resources

LIKE

- Social media
- About us
- Testimonials
- FAQs
- Guarantees
- Demos
- Trials
- Webinars
- Newsletters
- Endorsements

TRUST

- Contact us
- Inquire
- Buy now

CUSTOMERS

75%
LOOKING FOR
INFORMATION

23%
COMPARING YOUR
SERVICES TO OTHERS

2%
READY TO
TAKE ACTION

Social Media

The benefits of social media are many in terms of building name recognition and social proof. But the drawbacks are that, to do it right, it takes a lot of time, creativity, and money, and it ultimately is not a high return-on-investment strategy. As I mentioned before, your marketing efforts (social media in this case) act as a supplement to having good, consistent conversations – never as a replacement for them.

In terms of content, consider how best to use the content you produce to get the most mileage out of it. Think of it as a circle. If you've just written a blog, you could use the blog as your script on Facebook Live, or as a Facebook post. You can link to it in your email newsletter. You can write a "white sheet" or tip sheet about the topic, and let people know on social media that it's available. The order doesn't matter; what matters is how much you are able to use what you have produced.

There are many different social media channels – too many to have an active presence on all of them. Our advice is to focus on the two or three that most closely fit your ideal clients' profiles.

Facebook Groups help you build a community and give freely. When you're creating a group, think of a name for the group using words that make sense to your ideal client. And it's fine to invite your friends, family, and coworkers to "like" your group and join in if they wish.

The focus should be on creating excellent content, not on making a sales pitch. In our Facebook group, specifically for financial coaches, we let people know about our Financial Coaching Symposium, our Financial Coach Academy, and so on. But the primary focus is on solid, valuable content and conversations. You can offer tips, blog posts, or just invite and facilitate conversations between members. Articles from other sources that you think people might find valuable – new statistics about money management, a report on student loan debt – also are good options.

Finding Content

How to find content to recommend or link to? One valuable resource is Feedly.com, an aggregator of blog posts by topic. You can set up your Feedly account to receive any new blog posts about financial topics, for instance. Feedly has a free basic membership, or a "Pro" version that, at the time of this publication, costs $45 per year.

And if you like particular experts or companies, sign up for their email lists. You never know what might come in that's worth sharing, or that will spark your own ideas.

The rule is that for every ten posts you make, only one should include a sales pitch.

To the best of social media experts' knowledge, the current Facebook algorithm favors posts that foster genuine engagement and meaningful social interaction – posts that receive more shares, likes, and comments. For small businesses, this means your video content should encourage dialogue between users.

In our experience, posting a video generates far more engagement – that is, more views and more comments – than a written post of the same content. We've found that short educational videos about a particular topic and going live for an "AMA" or "Ask Me Anything" gets good engagement. At the end of your video, feel free to ask for "likes" and shares – if it's live, ask right then for a "heart" or a smiley face if folks agree with you.

We might create a GIF (Graphic Interchange Format), which is a soundless snippet of video that plays without anyone having to click on anything. Or we'll post a colorful graphic containing a question that prompts a "food for thought" type of reaction: *"If money were no object, would you rather have a housekeeper or a personal chef?"* In less

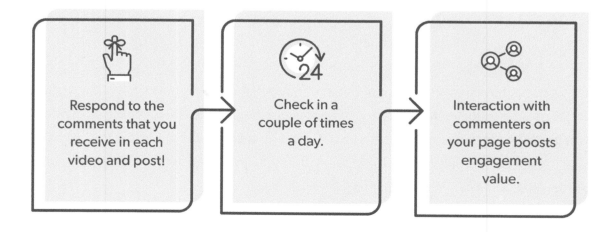

| Respond to the comments that you receive in each video and post! | Check in a couple of times a day. | Interaction with commenters on your page boosts engagement value. |

than a day, we reached more than 2,500 people with that one, and prompted 50 or 60 comments.

On social media, and even in our email campaigns, we always give people easy ways to offer testimonials: Yelp, Facebook, Google. In Google, you have to have a business account in order to do this, but it isn't difficult to set up.

We also ask for influencer endorsements. If there's a local business coach or someone who's great on Instagram who likes us and would be willing to send out a post mentioning that, it helps build name and brand recognition.

> "Content is anything that adds value to the reader's life."
>
> – AVINASH KAUSHIK,
> ENTREPRENEUR, AUTHOR, PUBLIC SPEAKER

Other Social Media Options

The same videos that you record for Facebook, or do live on Facebook, can be posted on YouTube. It's simple to do, and once again, it's a way to use the content you're creating to its best effect.

Twitter is not something we use a lot, but the social media management software we use allows us to post things on Twitter, so we do. I wouldn't say we get a lot of clients this way, but it is a speedy method for sharing tips, interesting articles, statistics, and so on. You can also share links to your videos that you've posted on other channels. Keep in mind, what works for our business and target demographic may not work for you and vice versa. If your market is on Twitter, then focus on that channel.

Pinterest is an easy way to drive people to your blog or website. Write a blog or article, go to the free design site Canva (mentioned in Chapter 4) to create an image to go with the article, share it as a "Pin" in your Pinterest account, and you're out there! The Pinterest post we've gotten the most traction from is on how to budget.

Using LinkedIn is one of the best methods for creating social proof that is meaningful to referral partners. Having a LinkedIn profile is a must for business people. Writing and posting thoughtful articles in this space, as well as joining groups, allows you to create conversations. You don't have to purchase the deluxe version, LinkedIn Premium, except that it permits you to send internal messages to anyone on LinkedIn, even if you aren't connected. That can come in handy.

Connecting Through LinkedIn

LinkedIn is also one of the best ways to reach out to potential referral partners to set up that initial one-on-one meeting. You can search the site by job title, such as "financial advisors" near you, and then send them a private message.

Here's a basic message template we use that has gotten the most responses:

"Hi [Name], thanks for connecting! Looking at your LinkedIn, I think there might be some areas where our worlds overlap regarding financial wellness. I'd like to find some time to explore this overlap over coffee, via Zoom, or on the phone. Please let me know what you think!"

As popular as it is, Instagram involves a somewhat crazy amount of work in order to establish and maintain a presence there, including staying online for at least 30 minutes after a post in order to be available to respond. Unless you're already active on Instagram, the payoff isn't that great for financial coaching.

Once you get your social media presence up and running, you should not have to spend more than an hour a week on it. Remember, the more you post is not necessarily better.

. . . .

Buffer is what we use to manage our social media posting at Fiscal Fitness Phoenix. It links to all our social media programs. You can upload what you want to post and schedule exactly when it will post – again, saving time. The least costly Buffer account is $15 per month at the time of this publication.

. . . .

HootSuite is another site with similar functions and capabilities, and it offers a free account.

In short, there's a ton of online technology out there to help create and organize your social media presence. Check it out and make good use of it!

30-Minute Marketing Ideas

Now that we've whetted your appetite for marketing your financial coaching business don't assume you can only do it if you block out large chunks of time. You can be just as effective with microbursts of time and energy! Create a calendar and put one of these items on it every day to ensure steady progress in getting the word out about your services.

☐ Write a blog (300 - 400 words)   ☐ Ask for an introduction

☐ Get a speaking gig   ☐ Host a webinar

☐ Create a checklist   ☐ Follow up with a prospect

☐ Sponsor an event   ☐ Attend a networking event

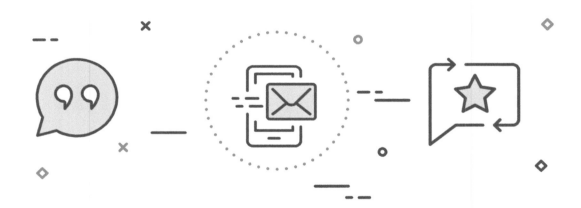

☐ Send a thank-you card   ☐ Write your biography

☐ Host a Facebook LIVE   ☐ Host a seasonal special

☐ Give a testimonial   ☐ Shoot a LIVE video

☐ Ask for a testimonial   ☐ Clear the office clutter

☐ Offer a VIP day   ☐ Send a nine-word email

- [ ] Invite people to a strategy session
- [ ] Make a high-end, one-for-one offer
- [ ] Track leads using Pipedrive (or another system)
- [ ] Celebrate your marketing efforts!
- [ ] Host a "Let's Make An Introduction" event
- [ ] Decide on a title for your signature talk

- [ ] Decide on a title for your signature talk
- [ ] Send a creative surprise to hot prospects
- [ ] List 10 podcasts on which you'd like to be guest
- [ ] Create a list of prospects to follow up with
- [ ] Offer a free tool on social media
- [ ] Call or email six places or groups where you could be a speaker

Chapter 05

Action Summary

☐ 1. Identify what you feel you are good at as a financial coach.

☐ 2. Become skilled at networking:

    a. Choose local organizations where you can connect with others.

    b. Consider a referral program for clients.

    c. Make a list of potential referral partners.

☐ 3. Make a list of local journalists or TV news producers and reach out with ideas.

☐ 4. Identify a potential lead magnet or freebie for your website.

☐ 5. Establish any social media profiles you desire and begin creating content.

☐ 6. Schedule out some of the 30-minute marketing ideas and add them to your calendar.

☐ 7. Complete the worksheet for Identifying Your Ideal Referral Partner. You can find it online at: https://www.financial coachacademy.com/idealreferralpartner.

DON'T *Worry*

about internet prospects
an internet galaxy away.

START *with the*

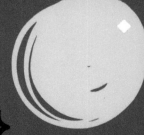

prospects in your
own backyard.

• ANGELIQUE REWERS •

The values exercise has helped me with couples who didn't think they were on the same page. I wasn't even thinking about all of these aspects of financial coaching so it helped to open up my eyes beyond the number.

SHERRY ANDREW

MONEY MINDSET FINANCIAL COACHING

Chapter 06

Financial Concepts - Feelings & Fears

For many people, money is a super-charged topic. Their family history and their feelings of self-worth are all tied up in their ability to make a living, support their families, and get ahead in their careers.

Sometimes as a financial coach, you will ask what seems to be a straightforward question that really seems to hit a nerve, maybe even prompting tears. Or you will see people hit what they perceive as a roadblock that you'll need to help them think differently about in order to navigate it and move forward.

In other words, there's a fair amount of psychology involved in good financial coaching. In this chapter, we'll cover financial feelings and fears. This includes how to ask effective questions in coaching sessions, as part of getting people to think not just about their bank balance or debt load, but about their overall financial philosophy.

I'll share some tips on overcoming procrastination, good exercises for getting clients to reflect on their feelings about money, and strategies for dealing with clients whose situations might be especially challenging.

Components Of Effective Coaching

Now let's discuss your roles in the coaching sessions – yes, there's more than one role! Using the same method I developed for creating client content, I've broken down the coaching process for a client meeting into steps that we can discuss individually:

Listen.

While it is important to have systems in place to keep the client meeting moving along and get certain things accomplished during the allotted time, it is just as important to be a bit flexible. In every client interaction, listening helps you know how to proceed. When you take your cues from the client – and this includes visual cues – you'll soon sense when you might be pushing too hard, whether their motivation seems to be waning or their frustration level is on the rise. Are they on overload, or are they ready to willingly take on more?

What you don't want is for the client to give up. Coaching is a delicate balance: allow your clients to learn and grow at their own pace while consistently challenging them to commit to certain steps, changes, and timelines. By really listening, you're also giving them permission to be honest with you about how they're feeling at that point.

Observing physical cues is one reason I advocate scheduling video appointments if you can't meet with a client in person, at least at first. Phone meetings might come later, but it's important that they see you – and vice versa – as they learn to trust you.

 Ask questions.

The questions you ask should get the client thinking through things on their own, to reflect on their situation and be able to talk through it with you. That's why you should avoid "yes/no" questions and ask those that require more detailed answers. In the next section of this chapter, we'll delve into specifics about asking good questions.

 Brainstorm solutions; educate.

Please don't gloss over this step, particularly as a new coach. The tendency is to get a bunch of information from the client and then feel you must present them with a tidy plan, already thought out. This bypasses the very valuable process of give-and-take, which builds trust and shows the client that you're open-minded and flexible. You'll bounce an idea off them – and you expect them to do the same.

You might know already what option you think would be best for them, but there's always more than one way to solve a problem. Brainstorming provides incredible insight into the client. And if they tell you they don't like an idea you've proposed, never take it personally. Get comfortable with hearing "no" once in a while. It is an indication that they're comfortable being honest with you.

Challenge the client to commit.

It's natural to assume this means wanting the client to commit to making changes or taking a particular action by a certain time. But there are so many other prospective areas of "commitment." I might ask the client to commit to staying positive if they're facing a big hurdle; or commit to trying again if the first time doesn't work as well as we'd hoped.

They can commit to not settling for an outcome less than what they want. This comes up when there's a job promotion or pay raise on the line, or sometimes a family situation, where everybody's expected to chip in to pay for a big gift or event.

I'll ask a question like, *"What would your ideal outcome be? Whether it's possible or practical isn't the point here – what would you love to see?"* From there, I'll ask, *"What is the bare minimum you would be willing to accept and still consider it a good outcome?"* This allows me to then urge them to not commit to anything less; to advocate for themselves.

· ·

No matter what the commitment, have the client put it in writing.

This simple act sets an intention and reinforces the conversation. If it's a deadline or a goal that requires reminders, ask them to add it to their calendar.

One situation you may run across is the client who is almost too committed – too ambitious, too early. How can this be a problem? Your instincts will tell you they can't maintain that level forever, and you don't want them to. Your focus may have to shift a bit, to get them to realize the benefits of a more manageable pace and calmer energy level, or they'll fizzle out. You can set deadlines that aren't as urgent for this type of client.

Effective Coaching Questions

Remember, your primary role is to listen. But you'll also need to ask questions that prompt client self-reflection and productive dialogue. Here are some questions I've found helpful:

For kicking off the client meetings:

- *What did you like this past week (about what we've done so far)?*

- *What didn't you like this past week?*

- *What worked well and what didn't go so well?*

- *Have you had any surprising observations this week?*

- *How often were you 'in your budget' and 'in your bank?'*

- *How would you score your own effort this week, on a scale of 1-10?*

- *Any other feedback from the week about what you're thinking, feeling, or doing that you'd like me to know about?*

Asking them for feedback underscores the fact that you're on this journey with them, no matter if it was a tough week. *"If you didn't like it, let's talk about it."* Make it clear that you don't expect to hear only good news. You can also give them a chance to brag a little if things went well, and tell them you're proud of their effort.

For breaking down a problem and updating our attempts to fix it:

- *What have you tried already?*

- *Is there any part of this attempt that worked well?*

- *Which part of this attempt did not work?*

- *How long did we try that solution before deciding it didn't work?*

Oftentimes, making a change or seeing results takes time, so it may just be that we need to stick with a strategy a little bit longer. But it's also important to pinpoint what DID work, and not settle for clients making statements like, *"The whole thing was a bust."*

For brainstorming new ideas:

- *What if we tried…? (Or, 'Have you tried …?')*

- *What can we learn from this situation?*

- *If it happens again, what would you do differently?*

- *If it happens again, what would you do the same? (In other words, what did you do right?)*

- *How long should we try this before deciding it isn't working?*

- *Is this something you can better plan for going forward?*

For questions like these, the tone is important. Make sure not to sound like you're lecturing or coming off like someone's stern parent! The idea is to reinforce that when people feel guilty or out of control about their finances, there are positive steps they can take to prevent that.

For challenging a client's assumptions or thoughts:

- *Where is that idea coming from?*

You'll need this question more than you might expect. So often, a client will make a very broad statement about the world, or work, or money – or themselves. They'll say, *"I can't do anything right."* Or, *"I'm so broke."* Or, *"It's the economy."* You're in a position to help them stop making the kinds of negative comments that can drag them down and stall their progress.

Which leads to the next question:

- *Did you use the budget to make that determination, or are you just guessing?*

Oftentimes, the financial picture just doesn't back up what they're saying. *"I totally messed up this weekend."* How do they know that? Look at their budget with them. They may be operating on old or invalid assumptions, and you can help them to see that.

- *"Let's look together and see if we can figure this out."*

This is what I say when a client asks, *"Can I buy…?"* and names a particular (generally high-dollar) item, or *"Can I go on a vacation this year?"* My goal is to show them how to make these decisions themselves – it's not my place to say yes or no! So, we look at the budget together and "pretend" that it's happening – and let them decide how feasible it is, or what they need to work on to make it feasible.

For inviting the client to share their thoughts about a new idea:

- *What did you hear during this conversation that was valuable or important to you?*

- *Share with me what you're thinking or feeling right now as we discuss this idea/topic.*

These discussions are also a good way to shore up the client who is feeling overwhelmed, or who assumes he or she must be doing "worse" than anyone else who's ever been coached. These kinds of blanket statements are your clues that they need a little more attention and, if they're excelling at any part of the process, it's time to point that out to them.

Goal-Setting

I like clients to pick one goal at a time. My feeling is that when it comes to financial goals, the strategy of "divide and conquer" doesn't work well. You end up dividing your money to throw, for example, at multiple credit card balances and making slower progress on each debt than you had hoped.

Which goal to pick? We evaluate all the financial aspects of each choice first, and if we're still unsure which one is best or which to do first, then I ask the client, *"Which goal excites you the most?"* The same is true whether it's putting money into savings, paying off debt, saving for a vacation or new furniture. They'll be more motivated and achieve their goals faster if it's something that really excites them.

We select a **target date** for achieving the goal, and also a range of outcomes: good, better, and best.

GOOD GOAL

Should be somewhat easy to attain. Something really bad would have to happen – a job loss, an unexpected serious illness – for the client not to hit this goal by the target date.

BETTER GOAL

This is a stretch. It moves the target date up by, say, a month.

BEST GOAL

Feels virtually impossible when you first set it, considering the budget you have to work with. It moves the target date up even earlier!

By setting these different levels of goals, the client will not see this as a pass-or-fail exercise.

Why even set a "best" goal that's pretty much irrational? Well, when your client hits it, their feeling of accomplishment is amazing. If you allow clients to set only those goals that they're sure to attain, they will never have the perspective of truly stretching and working for something better. I can't tell you how often it happens because it's more than you would expect. I'm still in disbelief! But I can tell you it's truly remarkable when a client sets a goal that feels impossible and then it happens!

The Goal-Setting exercise on the next few pages gives you an outline for discussion points with the client in determining their good, better, and best goals. It should prompt an honest assessment of exactly how they'll go about reaching the goal, what situations might get in the way and how they'll handle those obstacles, and even what they'll do to reward themselves when they've met the goal.

Goal-Setting Exercise

My #1 Goal is:

Target Date	Good	Better	Best

Write your action steps to this goal below:

1.

2.

3.

4.

5.

This goal is important to me because:

Obstacles that may arise include:

I plan on responding to such obstacles by:

After I reach my goal I will reward myself by:

After this goal is met, the next goal I will work on is:

Meaningful Exercises

You will sometimes find that when people are in the middle of a goal that takes a long time to achieve, or that they've lost some excitement about, they will need a pep talk to remind them just how far they've come. I call this a Reflection Exercise.

Let's say they've made a statement that represents a huge shift in the way they think about money. I might say, *"I'd like to take a moment to observe and appreciate what just happened. I want to compare what you said just now, to what you said when you first came in."* (You have their initial questionnaires from the Discovery Session, so you can quote them!)

You can ask some of the same questions that were on their initial paperwork *(How are you feeling about money? How stressed, or how confident, are you?)*, and compare the new answers to what they said initially. I sometimes pull up a couple's initial budget and compare it with their current one.

This almost always reveals and reinforces the growth they have experienced. It can be a powerful tool to keep them motivated. A bonus: It also does a heck of a lot to fuel your own sense of purpose as a financial coach.

Another insightful activity, both for client and coach, is what we call the Three Values Exercise.

> ... our values serve as our internal compass.

For most people, our values serve as our internal compass. Unfortunately, with all the world's distractions, many of us aren't keeping our values at the forefront anymore. They get buried beneath the expectations and values of others, the weight of social conformity, false beliefs, and even some of the messages and lessons we learned during our upbringing.

I can help people more effectively if I understand their values. And I've noticed that the clients who are aware of and confident about their value system, and spend money according to their value system, are happier and more grateful overall. I ask clients to list their top three values.

When you're working with a couple, have the two partners identify their top three values separately, and then compare them. You'll find it's not uncommon that two of the three are identical.

Remember, values are not things (like money) or actions (like running). Values are the needs that a person is able to fulfill with those things (money = security) or actions (running = health).

I use a list to prompt the client's thought process, but it is by no means complete:

Adventure	Freedom	Personal Growth
Appearance	Friendship	Pleasure/Play
Belonging	Generosity	Prosperity
Career Achievement	God	Recognition
Charity	Health	Security
Community	Impact	Spiritual Growth
Environment	Integrity	Travel
Family	Knowledge	Wealth

That's a lot to think about! But when our behavior is consistent with our values, we feel contentment, satisfaction, and internal strength. When our behavior is misaligned with our values, we feel lethargic, depressed, frustrated, even angry – and often without purpose.

Of course, there is no way that a person's budget can be allocated entirely to things that align with their values – it just isn't possible. However, we can try to make sure that the things that are most important to you are satisfied first.

No matter how much money I have or how many things I am able to purchase, if I'm not spending it on the right things for me, I won't be happy. But what happens to many people is they spend money on a lot of things that aren't important to them and then tell themselves they can't afford the things that are important to them.

The Three Values Exercise is designed to get a client thinking about life in a bigger way and not only financially. *"You're 100 years old, looking back on your life, what do you want to say you spent your time, money, and energy on?"*

This exercise has a definite financial component, which becomes clear as you delve into their answers. People often end up abandoning values they hold dear in order to prioritize (and pay for) other things.

You can ask the client(s):

- *Are any of the values that you've chosen completely unsatisfied or underfunded at the moment?*

- *If so, how can we get more resources working to fund this value?*
  By "resources," I don't necessarily mean money. Sometimes, what may be required is dedicating more time or energy to it.

- *Is there anything we can do to redirect some money to satisfy one of your values?*

- *If someone else saw your spending, your budget, or how you spend your days, would they be able to tell what your value system is?*
  (In other words, are you "walking the walk?")

- *How does your current goal support your values?*

For homework, I'll ask the clients to look at their budget and highlight anything that is not in some way aligning with one of their values. That doesn't mean I'm going to ask them to cut that expense! It just means we're going to be questioning it more often than an expenditure that better supports one of their values.

As a coach, think about how your business would feel every day if all your clients shared the same value system as you. On the other hand, imagine what it would be like if you found yourself routinely working with people with very different values than yours.

There are no right or wrong answers in the Three Values Exercise. But sometimes, it can provide valuable insight about why you relate better to some clients than others. That also can help you coach them more effectively.

Fighting Procrastination

You're asking clients to take "effective action," which means even if they learn something or try something that ends up not being especially useful, they've still learned or tried it. This means they've eliminated one of their choices and can choose another action, thereby narrowing down the right solution.

You will find that some clients are highly motivated in other areas of their lives and good at taking effective action – but they drag their feet when it comes to financial issues. Money avoidance is a real thing! You can diplomatically help them see this and work to change it.

What happens, for instance, when a client hasn't done anything you asked? Sometimes you cut the session short and give them the time to work on what they need to do to catch up. But sometimes, it will be necessary to talk about what might be causing the delay and help them address it. It's a signal of a potential block for them, and they need you to help them see it more clearly and support them as they work through it.

Too many times, coaches are tempted to "fire" a client who isn't keeping up with the assignments, instead of helping them see what might be causing that behavior.

Perhaps the procrastinator needs your help in completing the exercises you're giving them, until they gain more confidence in their own abilities. Maybe they aren't even aware of how they're avoiding these steps. Either way, it's the perfect opportunity to dive into it with them. There will be a section on Coaching in Challenging Situations later in this chapter that should help too.

A client has to learn to recognize their own "distractions" in this learning process. Do they find themselves cleaning or doing dishes when it's time to work on the budget exercises you've given them? Do they binge-watch a Netflix series or surf around on social media?

Remember, these behaviors are only the symptoms. Together, you can probe their underlying cause. Is it fear? Lack of time? Confusion or indecision? Are they simply too busy to focus? I ask, *"Do any of these sound familiar to you? Do you see yourself doing any of these?"* I might even have the client list them on paper instead of discussing them directly, which allows a bit of time for their own self-reflection.

Based on their answers, here are some strategies I suggest to them for getting past these obstacles to progress:

Time: Block off time for what I call "massive action" on your calendar. Block off time each morning to work on your budget. Make an effort to plan ahead. Set a minimum number of hours that you'll commit to it, each day or every week. Set deadlines for each action and goal.

Fear: Identify what you're afraid of, then focus on the fact that moving past this fear is the only thing that will actually achieve the results you seek. You simply cannot get results without taking action.

Confusion: Saying you don't know what to do or how to do something may be the biggest goal-crusher ever. Avoid it altogether by asking yourself, *"What do I know? Who do I know that can help me? What action can I take now, despite not having total clarity?"*

Overwhelmed: Free will and limitless options seem like a good thing, right? But they can paralyze you. Constraint and decision-making are the keys here. Narrow down your options to 2 or 3, then choose one. In some cases, setting a budget may automatically limit your options. And remind yourself that, in most instances, you can always change your mind later.

Too busy: People make time for the things that are truly important to them. Try reframing this by saying, "I didn't want to do it enough" – because if you did, you would have found the time. Take ownership of this choice and see if your mindset shifts. Or imagine that your tombstone reads, *"I was just too busy to... take action toward my dreams, create a life I really enjoyed, commit and follow through on financial fitness."*

Other "tough love" questions to pose for procrastinators:

- *What have I learned recently that I have not yet applied?*
- *What is stopping me from taking effective action and how can I overcome these obstacles?*
- *What commitments can I make to myself so that I can move toward these goals?*

For you as a financial coach, it's also important to check your own distractions. Look at your calendar at the end of the week and ask yourself, *"How much time did I spend reading versus doing? Talking versus taking action? Consuming versus creating? What are some daily actions I can take to get the results I seek and move me closer to my own goals? Weekly actions? Monthly actions?"*

> "The answer to procrastination is courage."
>
> – DAN SULLIVAN, THE STRATEGIC COACH, INC.

Financial Principles

When clients are enmeshed in the process of figuring out that they can be good with money, it's too soon to do this exercise with them. This one is for clients who've built up some confidence about their financial skills. Ask them to examine their financial principles. What rules do they live by in managing their money? Many folks already have financial principles; they just don't realize it or perhaps have never stated them outright.

> Many folks already have financial principles; they just don't realize it.

For instance, some people tithe a certain amount to their church. It is a non-negotiable number in their budget, and they feel strongly about it.

The person who defines their own financial principles is saying, *"I don't care what the trends are or what my friends say. This is how I'm going to make my own financial decisions – for the rest of my life."*

An excellent financial principle to decide on is whether you will loan money to family or friends. If the answer is yes, is there a limit on what you will loan? Are there specifics for paying it back in a timely manner? Would you agree to give a person money with no expectation of getting it back? If so, what's your limit? Knowing these principles and sticking to them can give you a great deal of peace of mind.

It is especially important for couples to be aware of each other's financial principles. This way, when one of their relatives calls to ask for a loan, it doesn't spark conflict. The time to have this conversation is when there are no emotions attached to it.

Other options for financial principles are:

- *Deciding to wait a certain length of time before making a purchase over a certain dollar amount. And this looks different depending on the value of the item being purchased! A $70 pair of jeans might require a "waiting period" of two days. A $25,000 car? More like two weeks, based on the amount of research you should be doing in advance.*

- *I must have the funds available in savings before I make any purchase that is considered a luxury.*

- *I am willing to go into debt for _____. This might be a house. Or a house and a car. Or a house, a car, and medical bills.*

- *Setting parameters for big purchases, like a home or vehicle. This means the maximum length of loan, interest rate, monthly payment amount, down payment, and so on, that you'd agree to not exceed.*

- *If I use a credit card for a purchase, I will have it paid off within ___ (number of days).*

- *I will not pay more than ____ percent interest on a credit card.*

For couples: *We will discuss any purchase or transaction over a certain dollar amount. Michael and I have a rule that for any purchase over $1,000, we have to wait over a weekend before we make the decision. We found ourselves making a big purchase on a weekend – and then rethinking it on Monday when we're back on the job and thinking about how hard we work for our money!*

My emergency savings will never drop below $ _____.

My emergency savings can only be used for _____.
(Make this list as specific as possible).

I will invest a minimum of _____ % of income each year in _____.
(My retirement account, long-term financial health, investments, etc.).

You can strengthen a principle, but when you're in the middle of a transaction or the research for a transaction, you cannot change your principle. You must honor it. From a financial coaching perspective, whatever is on the financial principles list cannot be renegotiated. The clients want to trim their investment percentage to take a vacation? That violates their principles.

Here is perhaps the ultimate financial principle:

I/We will always live on $_____ or less per year. This helps to prevent what is often called "lifestyle creep" – people make more money, so they spend more money. Eventually, their income might have doubled but they're still barely getting by.

This is the most difficult principle to live by, in my view. As you become more successful, it is natural to want more flexibility in your budget. You can certainly spend a little more if you make a little more – as long as you realize it's not an open door and an endless flow of "extra" cash.

The clients I've worked with who set that annual maximum-budget dollar amount are the ones who, today, are able to save 30 percent or more of their income.

My final suggestion for a financial principle is one I wish everyone would adopt:

> *I will take ownership and personal responsibility for my finances. I will advocate for myself and stay engaged and curious about money topics.*

We stick to our principles even when it's inconvenient – in fact, especially when it's inconvenient. And these can become a cornerstone of the financial coaching process, guiding how a person makes wise financial choices throughout life. When a client comes to me in the middle of a decision-making process, and I know they've written out their principles, the first question I ask is, *"How does this align with your principles?"*

Coaching In Challenging Situations

It is important that you have a structure and procedures in place, but also that you maintain some flexibility in working with clients. If you're facing a client who's resisting your questions or advice, showing a lot of tension or frustration, or you're simply not feeling good about how a session is going – I believe it is best to be pleasant but firm as you tee up the idea of continuing the discussion at a later date.

I might say:

- *There's something I'm observing right now, but I can't quite put my finger on it...*

- *There's something I don't like about this scenario...*

- *There's a way we can do this, but I feel like I need to think on it for a bit.*

- *I need to let this challenge simmer, and I'll get back to you on it.*

- *I want to do some more research before I make any recommendations.*

Sometimes, it's best to hit "reset" and continue on a different path or at a different time, when the client might be more receptive. It also might be true that you need to do a little more digging to help them tackle an issue in their financial life. Either way, be as honest with the client as you expect them to be with you.

Reading Recommendations

BOOK TITLE	AUTHOR	INSIGHT
Business Storytelling for Dummies	Dr. Karen Dietz	For marketing and understanding how to tell a story with your brand and who you are as a coach, these are both great.
Building a Storybrand	Donald Miller	
Start With Why	Simon Sinek	Helping you get to the heart of WHY you are who you are and how that can be a powerful foundation for your business; these books by Simon Sinek are my go-to.
Find Your Why		
The Power of Vulnerability	Brené Brown	As a coach, if being vulnerable with clients is challenging for you, let me suggest reading some of Brené Brown's books. They are great for helping you to understand empathy and compassion as a coach. They also help with encouraging bravery and vulnerability as an entrepreneur.
Dare to Lead		
Daring Greatly		
Profit First	Mike Michalowicz	Perfect for your own business finances and if you plan to coach small business owners.
12-Week Year	Brian Moran	Goal-setting is important, and this book by Brian Moran is my top recommendation for setting your goals.

BOOK TITLE	AUTHOR	INSIGHT
Facilitating Financial Health	Brad Klontz	This is a must-read to expand your coaching skills!
It's Not About the Money	Brent Kessel	This is great for money mindset.
Your Money or Your Life	Vicki Robin	Both are beautiful foundational books on personal finance - I recommend them to most clients.
I Will Teach You to Be Rich	Ramit Sethi	
How to Win Friends & Infuence People	Dale Carnegie	This is a timeless work, great for improving your communication skills and how you respond to people.

There are some especially challenging financial dynamics that you will come across, perhaps often, in your coaching.

I've divided them into eight specific situations, along with advice for each:

 Clients whose expenses far exceed their income.

I think for this client, a major role of the coach is to make them aware of the simple fact that they're spending more than they bring home – because it isn't so "simple."

Month-to-month, this person is constantly juggling and often assumes they're making poor spending choices or doing something wrong. So, imagine the clarity you're providing by offering proof that isn't the case. They're just not bringing in enough income.

The resulting choices are not easy, however. This client needs to do something significant and dramatic to make more money. Don't sugarcoat this. It might be taking on a second job, getting a roommate – at least for a while – selling a vehicle or some valuables.

It could be getting a better-paying job. Instead of a financial coach, you can suggest that this client seek out a career coach or résumé writer. Then later, after their financial life isn't in such immediate turmoil, they can come back and focus with you on budgeting, goal-setting, and so on.

Do not hesitate to urge them to take advantage of the community services that are available – from their church to local food pantries, utilities' payment plan options, even state services. United Way has a financial coaching program for lower-income individuals that might be a better fit for them.

Do not downplay the impact we can have by showing compassion in these stressful times and by directing the client to the resources that can best serve them.

 People who use credit cards for EVERYTHING.

Spending on a credit card typically leads to overspending, but not always. As a financial coach, how you personally feel about credit cards has everything to do with how you advise this client – or if you even take them on as a client to begin with.

If your philosophy about using credit conflicts with theirs, you're setting yourself up for a very challenging coaching experience.

In other words, if the prospective client puts everything on a credit card "to earn rewards points," and you believe credit cards should be used only for emergencies, those two outlooks are never going to jibe.

My own viewpoint is that credit cards aren't all bad – but when a client first comes in, I don't know yet if credit card use should or will be an option for them.

I haven't figured that out yet. So, I default to, "Not yet." My approach is to set up a system in which they don't use their cards for a few months, while we're establishing new habits. Then, we can start adding the credit cards back into their budget and designing a strategy for using them.

In short, they have to prove that they have earned the right to use a credit card. And you need to ask, *"Are you open to hearing about a different strategy?"*

I find it works best to have very strict procedures for credit card use. You set a dollar amount that you can put on the card – and you cannot put ONE MORE DOLLAR on that card. We decide exactly what they can use the card for and what they cannot use it for. We set a number of days by which the card balance must be paid off – yes, days. Not months!

For people who use a credit card for everyday expenses, I'll even have them pay it off every week, if that's what it takes to keep their budget on track.

A separate credit card must be used for the things that we save for: travel, clothing, car repairs. The client makes the purchase on the card, then withdraws the money from that specific savings account to pay it off within a certain number of days or within one week.

For those folks who are manic about earning points that can be redeemed, I suggest they redeem them for cash – and then put the cash to a truly responsible use. Apply it to their mortgage. Sock it away in their retirement account. We temporarily remove the thrill of earning more points to see the kind of spending decisions they make without them. Then, when the points are reintroduced, we can compare their decision-making with and without points.

For prospective coaches who support the use of rewards credit cards, let me explain: I find that most clients are not using their rewards points strategically when I first begin working with them. They also don't realize how inefficient they are at earning the points. So, I ask that they redeem the points for cash while we are putting them on a solid foundation of budgeting and planning. Only then do we dive into other strategies (such as the so-called Chase Gauntlet) and better ways to use their reward credit cards.

 Couples who keep their bills or accounts separate.

This is an interesting situation, and I try to find out what their overall vision is and why. Do they see themselves continuing to keep their personal finances separate, or do they want to combine them at some point?

I'm honest with them that the couples I work with who combine their income, expenses, and financial goals build wealth faster. There's more joint accountability, joint effort, a sense of teamwork, and mutual support. But in some cases – second or third marriages later in life, or when one person has children and the other does not – they're more comfortable keeping their finances separate. In my experience, it is tough to convince these couples to do otherwise, and my job is not to try and convince them they should want something they simply do not want for themselves. My hope is to help them put a system in place that honors their choices while supporting their goals.

In the coaching process, I ask each partner to commit to putting in similar effort. We can't have one following through and the other slacking off. Generally, you'll find one person is better at it than the other, but that isn't the point. They're in this together!

I create a budget for each – in separate tabs on the same spreadsheet, so there is full transparency. Otherwise, my goal is to help them set mutual and supportive goals and so on – and if there's extra money in their monthly budget, to consider combining that.

I also caution them that this is going to be a relationship we're building, and it cannot be done in a single coaching session. This is challenging, so I want them to know we have to work through it together over a period of time to implement it successfully.

If they decide they'd be willing to try combining their money, it's a big step. They need to feel like the process is fun or doable to start, and they might naturally assume that this will be taking away some of their flexibility or freedom – even their identity.

> They need to feel like the
> process is fun or doable...

The biggest fear for some is that when they really want to buy something, they'll have to ask permission. So, I usually give couples a timeline: *"Let's try it for four months, and if it doesn't work, we can reevaluate."* And I don't suggest that they commit the extra money in their budget to the drudgery of paying down a credit card or making an extra mortgage payment. Instead, those extra dollars can allow each some spending flexibility. This initial strategy can serve as a transition and ease some of the growing pains of such a significant change.

 People who have intermittent or variable income.

This type of budgeting is more challenging because it requires the client's critical thinking on a regular basis. Unlike most budgets, based on income that is the same every month, those with fluctuating income require different decisions and strategies.

Like the client we discussed earlier whose expenses far exceed their income, there's a basic level of frustration here. The person with variable pay often assumes they aren't doing things right, or they wouldn't feel so stretched all the time.

The starting point for this client is to determine a minimum amount that they need to make each month based on their bills, and create a budget based on this minimum income threshold. "Bills" include any expense – even if it isn't paid on a monthly basis *(ex. car insurance or registration)*.

Then, we create a "pecking order," by prioritizing what to do with the money that comes in during higher-income months. It's almost like having different levels of plans. Level One is the basic budget. Level Two is adding in "extra" (but still important) items, such as saving for clothing or travel or gifts –things that are needed from time to time and would otherwise be charged on a credit card. Level Three allows them to set goals for whenever they have money over and above what is needed for Level Two – such as paying off a credit card.

Sometimes, this approach will feel to the client like they're slogging along.

Progress can be very slow, and even nonexistent during months when income is low. It is critical that the client understands, even in the months they're not "making progress," they are MAINTAINING. They aren't backsliding or digging themselves into a deeper hole. That, in and of itself, is progress for someone with variable income.

I often use the concept of a deposit account with this type of client. Let's say we have determined that they need $5,000 a month for their basic budget.

Every bit of income to their household is deposited into a single account – then every month, they write themselves a "paycheck" of $5,000 and put it into a different bank account they use to pay their bills. This allows them to live month to month without drastic lifestyle changes or cutbacks; they always have enough to fund the basics and keep plugging along.

Of course, the deposit account might look wildly different month-to-month. But over time it should reflect the "extra" funds that they can use for their goals.

Important note: If this system does not allow them to maintain their $5,000 monthly draw for basic bills, it has revealed the real issue – a lack of sufficient income, not a faulty budgeting process or wayward spending habits.

For commission-based salespeople and entrepreneurs, just becoming aware of what they have to do is a powerful motivator. When they know they need to make more, it spurs them on to greater productivity, more sales calls, whatever it takes.

 The client who is an "over-giver."

This client might be giving money to charity, or "helping out" their grown children or grandchildren – all noble and understandable pursuits. However, when they're doing it at the expense of their own financial well-being, it should raise all kinds of red flags. Your job as a financial coach is to help them set boundaries or limits so they still are able to give and feel good about it without being taken advantage of.

You can start by creating a "giving fund" in their budget, either per family or per person. The idea is to create a cap on the amount they can give – quality over quantity!

This is one area in which the Three Values conversation can have significant impact. Their top three values probably include taking care of family, or "being there" for the grandkids' financial needs – but there are two other values, and those also require attention and money. Your job as a financial coach is not to tell people they "can't do this." What you can say is, *"I want you to do this while honoring the other things that are important to you."*

You might have to ask some tough questions: *"If your daughter knew that you went into debt to buy that for her, and if she knew how much stress this credit card debt is causing you – how do you think she'd feel about that? If she knew you were putting off your own goals to help her, do you think she would want you to do this?"*

You might also ask, *"How could you help your daughter in ways that aren't financial? Let's make sure there isn't a solution that would require no money before we spend yours in this way. Could we try that first?"*

Again, the point is not to make the over-giving client feel guilty or weak-willed for doing this. It's wonderful that they have a giving spirit and want to help. Our goal is to make structure around these expenditures, so the client can make their own financial progress at the same time. The client should feel good about their ability to give – not resentful about it.

 The former Discovery Session client whose sessions are over, but has hit a roadblock or challenge and has reconnected.

I handle these situations in much the same way as a Quick Audit and schedule it as a Next Steps consultation, which is a 15-minute call. I make sure to set expectations right up front: *"We've got 15 minutes; let's figure out how we can get you moving forward!"*

I also build rapport by thanking them for being courageous enough to call and ask for help: *"This is what I'm here for! I'm so excited to help you through making these changes and seeing results."*

From this point, the conversation is much like the Quick Audit. I ask them to give me an idea of the problems they're experiencing that they are hoping to solve. I make sure I've looked at their original worksheet/questionnaire, so I can refer to their goals and priorities – but what I need to know from this call is, what happened to derail their progress? Is it a time crunch, a lack of discipline, a financial emergency? I ask, *"Did you make any of the changes we talked about? How did they work for you?"* Give them a pat on the back if they did make some effort!

Based on their current situation and their goals, I then suggest the coaching program I think would be best for them. For return clients, it isn't about the process – they're familiar with the process. It's that some things are holding them back in their decision-making.

I reference a specific goal in making the "ask" – *"I know you want to (get out of debt, buy a house, be a lot less stressed with money). Based on that goal, I'm going to recommend (this program)."* I explain why it's the best fit, what they will gain from the program, how much it costs, and how they can get started. *"Here's where you can be in four months. What questions do you have about that?"*

I don't end with the price. I sandwich it into the details so they have a chance to process the information before I ask if they have questions.

If they're ready to continue, we set our first appointment. If they're not, there isn't anything more I can do for them, even as much as I know I can help them. The way I see it, if they have proven that they can't do it on their own – but they aren't willing to hire me as a coach, despite outlining all the benefits – they have made their choice. Clients have to WANT coaching.

 One spouse talks a lot – the other says nothing.

Try to engage them both. I'll ask a question and say (to the quiet one), *"Bob, I'd like you to answer first…"* If it's an in-person meeting, I'll turn and face the quiet person as I'm asking questions, so they feel my attentiveness and willingness to listen. (To a certain extent, this is possible even in an online call.) In a subtle way, this also blocks the more talkative person, which might reduce their interruptions or interjections.

I also try to ask a quieter client more open-ended questions, such as, *"What would you like to see from the budget?" "What do you need for this process to feel like it's a success for you?" "What role do you want to play with money?"* I will be very direct and say, *"You can tell me what you're thinking right now...I can take it!"* Let them know they can be honest with you and that you're not oblivious to their needs. You might have to pull their trust out of them, but it's important that they know they can share with you.

Let's say you're working with Tina and Bob, a married couple, and Tina is driving the conversation train, so to speak. You might say to her, *"Tina, I feel really comfortable in my understanding of what you want to accomplish – or what you think the problems are, or what you think has worked or didn't work well – but now, I want to gain that same understanding from Bob, so let's give him a moment to share, okay?"*

 The individual who is entrepreneurial-minded, but doesn't have immediate revenue to invest and therefore spends on credit.

For this client, it's all about putting the plan and timeline in place so they can see it's possible to meet their goals.

This person often just throws money at a problem because they feel an urgent need to deal with it and can't see that a longer-term improvement is possible.

There's a sense of immediate gratification – *"I'm doing something now for my business, although I have no clue about what's going to happen down the road."*

> Most times when people make
> poor decisions, it's because
> they don't see the alternative...

Most times when people make poor decisions, it's because they don't see the alternative. They don't see that making a short-term bad choice ultimately takes away from what they really want long-term.

And it's not always financial. I sometimes ask, *"What time or energy effort can you put into this that might have some results – instead of spending money on this problem? This might mean, who can you talk to? What connections can you make? What work can you put in as far as determining who your ideal client is, or what your business name would be, or designing a handout or flyer?"*

We might brainstorm five things they can do – all of which require no money – and they have to do all five of them before they can spend another dollar on their business.

Depending on the client's circumstances, the plan might include an amount that they need to have in savings before they can quit their "day job" to pursue their business, set a target date for submitting their resignation, or set a schedule for paying off their credit cards.

If there's no plan in place and no progress being made, the would-be entrepreneur just feels stifled and frustrated – and this can cause them to make poor money decisions, which then creates a vicious cycle that keeps them stuck.

In much the same way as the "over-giver," we want to honor this part of the entrepreneur's personality. But at the same time, we need to help them manage it in order to make headway on their goals.

Money Mindset

If I sense that a client has some deep-seated or intense blocks around money that are preventing them from taking some of the steps I'm proposing, I will wade into the topic of their money mindset.

For me, one resource that has been especially helpful in this area is *It's Not About the Money*, an excellent book by Brent Kessel (2009; HarperOne). Kessel delves into why and how some people are able to find peace of mind in any financial situation, while others struggle with it.

Kessel created a questionnaire, available on his website at AbacusWealth.com/Quiz, to help a person determine their money archetype. The quiz, along with information in the book, helps to pinpoint a client's money mindset, from guardian to pleasure-seeker, to idealist or caretaker. For some, it's a real eye-opener! I recommend his book to clients whom appear to continuously struggle with aligning their spiritual and financial lives.

Always Asking, Always Learning

The takeaway from all these examples should be that there's always a way to help people, although the solution you offer may not have an immediate impact. The plan might have a dozen steps, but it prioritizes their needs and helps guide the client through achieving them.

Oftentimes, newer coaches shy away from asking questions if they aren't sure of the answer. But in my view, it's the best thing you can do! If you assume you already know the answer, you're likely not listening effectively to your client.

As a new coach, it can be scary to ask a question you're not sure how they'll answer. What if you don't know what to say next? What if you haven't seen this problem before? What if you're not sure how to tackle that particular thought? As a result, we tend to ask questions only when we feel we're in control – and if that's the case, our clients' results will ultimately suffer.

Trust your ability to listen to the client. Trust your ability to help them, no matter their response. And as I've mentioned before, if you're not sure how to tackle something, say that! *"I'd like to think about this a bit more and get back to you."* Or, *"There's obviously more to unpack here, and I want to continue talking about it. Would that be okay?"*

I find these situations have made me a stronger coach. Challenge yourself to observe how many questions you're asking that you don't think you already know the answer to.

Chapter 06

Action Summary

☐ 1. Create a cheat sheet of effective questions so you can have it nearby during client sessions.

☐ 2. Think through your philosophy regarding the scenarios used in this chapter: variable income, credit card spending, the over-giver, couples, and expenses exceeding income.

☐ 3. Make a list of other scenarios you might come across and begin to think through how you might help the client to tackle those scenarios. Seek guidance and insights from other financial coaches or resources so you can feel more prepared.

☐ 4. Continue developing new exercises for your clients based on some of the financial concepts, fears, and feelings outlined in this chapter.

☐ 5. Prioritize the books in the "Recommended Reading" section with those that might expand your skills the most.

When we are in the process of creating SOMETHING we must have flexibility of mind to move WITH WHAT NEEDS to be done: what allows this to HAPPEN IS PRECISELY THE FACT WE'RE NOT ATTACHED TO how things should be done.

• COLIN POWELL •

My biggest takeaway was that there is a WEALTH of topics and skills I can teach clients. I'll never run out of things to guide them through as long as I take the time to reflect on how to best serve them and create exercises that will help my clients develop those skills. I have used the mindset that Kelsa encourages us to take on to continuously push myself to create new content that can serve my audience.

JACLYN WISE

THE WISE WAY

Chapter 07

Financial Concepts - Money & Budgeting

In this chapter, we'll delve into the "dollars and cents" of money management as opposed to the feelings and fears associated with it. One of the traits that makes you a "coach" instead of a financial planner is that you will be dealing with both of these aspects of your clients' relationship to their personal (or small business) finances.

To so many people, money is an abstract concept. They know how it influences things – you spend more this month, you have to find a way to pay it back next month – but all too often, it's more like a tangled cobweb. The common practice of paying some bills automatically and/or online seems to exacerbate the impression that money isn't tangible. It flies in and out of the bank account without much thought. People aren't sure where it's going and don't feel they are in control of it. This prompts feelings of stress and unhappiness.

> ... once a person can clearly see their money and where they stand financially, they will make better choices.

I believe that once a person can clearly see their money and where they stand financially, they will make better choices. It's my job to paint that picture for them in the Discovery Session. When I say "paint that picture," I mean make it visual. Give them something to look at and it will make your job as a coach so much easier.

The client can also see that what I'm showing them isn't my opinion. I can say, *"Do you see what I'm seeing? In your next paycheck, you'll have a little extra money. What do you want to do with it?"*

I never begin by telling people, *"You're spending too much here,"* or, *"You need to cut back there."* Rather, I might say, *"It looks like you're over budget by about $400 a month. Let's see where we can find that $400."*

With new clients, I know they often take steps to please me or make me proud of them. But when I know I'm succeeding with them is when I see them take steps to make themselves proud, because they care about their plan. That's a great moment!

Financial Skills

Some of the skills you'll be helping people develop will be used rarely, although they're important. Still others will be used every week or every month. But one of the most important skills is planning ahead.

When graphic novelist Stephen McCranie said, *"Failing to plan is like planning to fail,"* he wasn't kidding. Actually, the idea is even older than that – a similar iteration of that quote is widely attributed to Benjamin Franklin.

I've created multiple "tracker" spreadsheets that allow people to plan ahead for:

Travel

Medical Expenses

Subscriptions

Home Maintenance

Vehicle Maintenance

Holiday Gift Expenses

Are there others you can think of? Create them and use them!

The idea is, people feel more in control of their finances when they're not always reacting and scrambling – *"Oh, man, I forgot the car insurance is due in July. How are we gonna cover that?"* If you're going to have a tough month or two during the year, in which you know you'll have more expenses piling up, wouldn't you rather know in advance and plan for it? The ability and discipline to plan ahead can transform your attitude about money.

Planning Ahead By Month

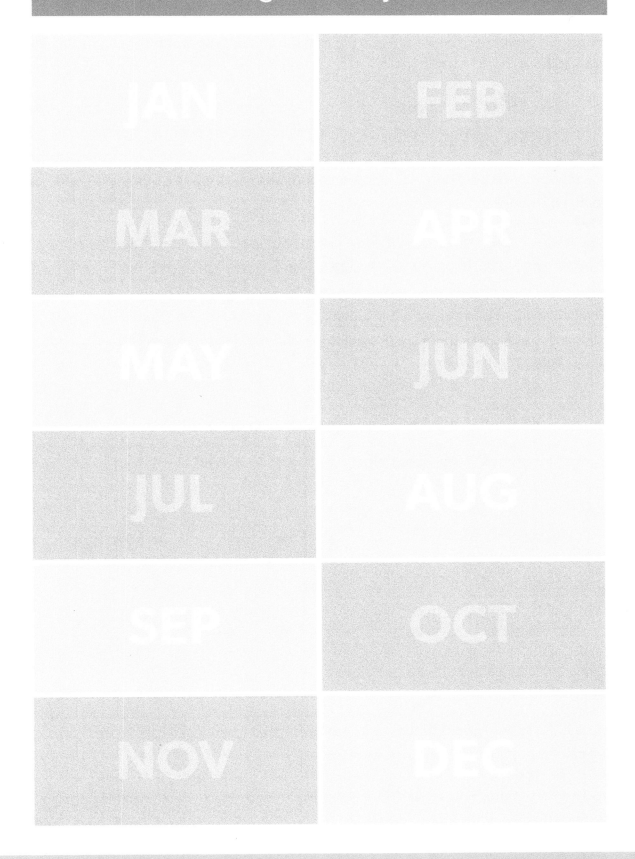

JAN

FEB

MAR

APR

MAY

JUN

JUL

AUG

SEP

OCT

NOV

DEC

Certain expenses tend to crop up year after year, but they aren't frequent so they tend to surprise people. For this, I offer a *Planning Ahead by Month* spreadsheet (see page 191) that helps people budget for these – from Mother's Day to school proms, to Halloween treats and costumes. People can add birthdays and their own events to customize their spreadsheet.

When I ask a client, *"What do you have coming up in the next week?"* it's amazing how many people can list work or events, but not their financial obligations. They simply don't see their activities in terms of money. And yet, won't their daughter need some cash for the school field trip? Won't they be paying for dinner when they take their girlfriend out for her birthday?

So, I start by asking them to plan for their financial needs one week out. Then, two weeks. Then, what's coming up in the next month? Eventually, they should be able to anticipate expenses three months out, and six months, and so on. It's like flexing a muscle so it will get stronger and stronger. Of course, it's impossible to anticipate every possible expense. But most of them are predictable – and their due dates will arrive, whether you're ready for them or not.

A New Way To Budget

The problems you're going to help most clients tackle are:

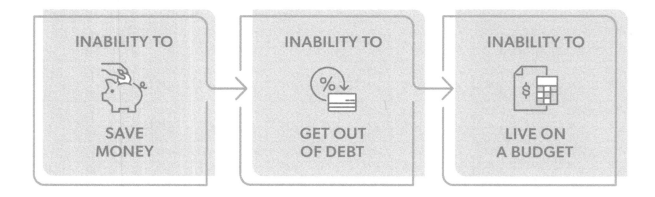

| INABILITY TO | INABILITY TO | INABILITY TO |
| SAVE MONEY | GET OUT OF DEBT | LIVE ON A BUDGET |

Here is the system and structure that I use to solve all three. At Fiscal Fitness Phoenix, we call it the Ultimate Financial Power Plan.

You might wonder why we opted to use this rather than any of the other budgeting systems that are easily found online – and if you have one you prefer, by all means, use it. But this system is the most visual representation we've been able to find to show a client's finances as a continuum: where they've been, where they are now, and where they're headed.

Many traditional budgets start with a person or a couple's income and a list of expenses. Subtract the monthly expenses from the monthly income and you see if you're covering them or not.

The trouble with this is, nobody lives their life that way. Life is not linear! Income and expenses ebb and flow through the month.

INCOME	ACTUAL
My income	$2,400.00
Spouse's Income	$2,400.00
Cash-back or Rewards	$25.00
Misc. Income	$0.00
Monthly Income Total	$4,825.00
EXPENSES	ACTUAL
Auto Loan	$350.00
Cash	$200.00
Cell Phone	$90.00
Credit Cards	$2,000.00
Daycare	$500.00
HOA Dues	$30.00
Insurance, Auto	$100.00
Insurance, Life	$60.00
Misc. Spending	$100.00
Mortgage	$1,200.00
TV • Internet • Phone	$125.00
Utilities • Gas, Electric	$250.00
Utilities • Water	$0.00
Monthly Expense Total	$5,005.00
Monthly Net Exchange	$180.00

If you put them on a basic graph, they'd look something like this:

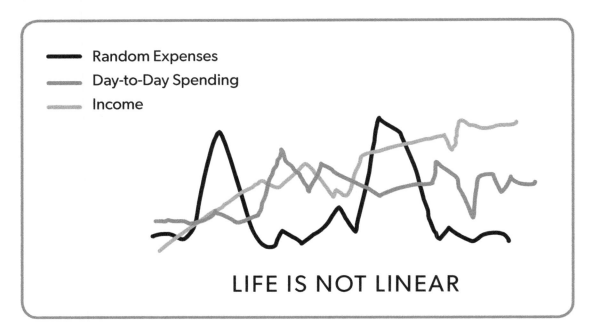

Random Expenses
Day-to-Day Spending
Income

LIFE IS NOT LINEAR

Random expenses that sneak up on most families: Home repairs, car repairs, clothing, gifts, or travel. These tend to be large expenses that are paid for with credit cards. Shown on a graph, it would be a line with big up-and-down swings.

Day-to-day spending: Eating out, dry cleaning, kids' field trips. These tend to be expenses that are paid with debit cards. On a graph, this line would also be "wavy," but with highs and lows not nearly as big as the random expenses.

Income: Interestingly, most people's income is not a flat, predictable line on our graph. Within a single month, it'll be flat for a while – then comes a BIG spike (a paycheck, or bonus, or tax refund). Then it's flat again, until the next spike.

The Ultimate Financial Power Plan prompts the client to organize things differently, starting with three categories:

Fixed, recurring expenses: These are the monthly bills that only vary in some cases (such as utility bills in summer or winter) and are typically due at the same time each month. These tend to cause the least amount of overall stress, primarily because they are expected.

Day-to-day spending: Groceries and eating out, entertainment, dry cleaning. Some folks include gas or transportation costs. As mentioned, these are typically debit card expenditures.

Random or non-recurring expenses: The car quits running, the air conditioner quits cooling. We know these will happen, but we never know when! Many people don't save for them or, if they do, it's in an emergency-fund type of account. In this category, we also include expenses that happen quarterly, biannually, or annually (car insurance or registration, license renewals, subscriptions or membership dues, etc.)

Let's look at each category separately.

Fixed, recurring expenses

If a monthly bill fluctuates somewhat – say, for water or electricity, it's between $120 and $150 – always estimate it at the higher amount. That allows a little padding as we create the new budget.

I find clients often group their bills by category (all home-related expenses, all car expenses), or by amounts, assuming that whatever amount is highest has to be paid first. Instead, I ask the client to list their accounts and amounts in the order of their due dates. This makes it easier for them to coordinate the timing of their bills and their paychecks.

Budgeting by paycheck is easier than budgeting by month. If one spouse gets paid in opposite weeks from the other, it's easy to decide which bills get paid with which paychecks, week to week.

Day-to-day expenses

I ask clients to estimate how much they think they'll need per pay period and to pay day-to-day expenses in cash – using their debit card ONLY for gas. People might grumble at first about having to carry and use cash, and that's understandable. But I explain that it's the best way to see their money more clearly and to turn all the "nickel-and-dime" purchases into a single, fixed expense that can be tracked and/or adjusted. I like to ask clients to try cash first and if after a few months, they still don't love it, I give them an alternative solution: to transfer the set amount on payday to a separate "spending checking account" where they can use a debit card.

If you're familiar with or have clients who have used the "cash envelope" method, they might have tried putting their cash in envelopes marked for different purposes. But we've found that folks who run out of cash in their "dining out" envelope will raid their "grocery" envelope. So, let's just make it a single amount that they can use as they wish to meet those day-to-day expenses without having to worry about where every dollar goes.

 Random, non-recurring expenses

These are the big peaks and valleys on our expense graph. The goal here is to smooth out the highs and lows and make this category perform more like fixed, recurring expenses.

Let's say a client knows her car insurance is going to cost $360 every six months. That's $60 a month, but she is billed twice a year. I'm going to ask her to set aside $60 a month.

Do the same for the new tires she knows she will need, and the oil changes the car receives every four months. Add up these smaller amounts and place that total, every month, in a savings account for Car Maintenance and Insurance. If the car is older and will need more substantial repairs – or if she'll be looking for a new car in the next year – there should be an amount saved monthly for repairs or a down-payment.

Where to set these funds aside? I like CapitalOne's "CapitalOne360" accounts or Ally, so that's what I currently recommend for these smaller, targeted savings accounts. (Neither of those companies rewards me in any way to recommend them.) You want an online bank with no fees, no minimum balances, and the best possible interest rate. While there are apps that offer "online buckets," we have found that having the actual savings accounts works best for our clients.

The client can set up as many accounts as they want, tied to their checking account so that they can transfer money. Home repair, vacation, travel (non-vacation), clothing, cars, education, or quarterly taxes (for self-employed people.) These are just a few savings account ideas. I ask the client to transfer a set amount of money on a set date, every month, to each of their targeted savings accounts.

If an expense arises in one of these areas, the client can pay with a credit card – then transfer the money out of that savings account into their checking account to pay off the credit card balance.

Why multiple, targeted savings accounts? I've found that people who have a single savings account for emergencies almost never feel good about actually having to take money out of it. They see it as a cushion that they have worked hard to amass, and it worries them to see the balance drop for any reason, no matter how valid.

Assigning savings amounts to specific purposes or goals makes sense because it gets the money out of the checking account. This minimizes the temptation to fritter it away on other expenses whenever the client sees "extra money" in checking. It really isn't extra money! It is money for which the bill hasn't yet come due or the need hasn't quite arrived. But it will.

Another benefit of multiple accounts is that the clients can see the balances build steadily for each goal they have set for themselves.

Some coaches we've trained use and recommend YNAB, short for *You Need A Budget*, personal budgeting software based on the "envelope method." It offers the ability to plan months ahead. There's a small fee after the free trial period.

 At Fiscal Fitness Phoenix, about one in five clients has an emergency fund when they first come to see us. By "emergency fund," I mean money in savings to be able to cover their expenses for three to six months in case they lose their job. Using this budgeting method, 85 percent have established and funded this type of savings.

To summarize, one of your most important goals as a financial coach is to show people how to use their money to fund their goals. Help them get off the stressful treadmill of "income and outflow" that seems out of their control.

By using the system I've just outlined, when true "extra" money comes in – a bonus, a tax refund, an extra paycheck on those three-paycheck months based on a typical year's calendar – the client is able to decide what to do with it to make the most progress toward their goals. That feels so much better than having to use it to catch up a big credit card balance.

We set up the new budget on an Excel spreadsheet that allows the client to forecast for several months at a time, making it even easier to experiment (onscreen) with the amounts they allocate to different debts or savings priorities.

The "New Normal" For Budgeting And Bill-Paying

As mentioned, the goal of the new budget is to even out the highs and lows caused by random, non-recurring expenses. Now, every month is more predictable. When a paycheck comes in, the client follows these few simple steps:

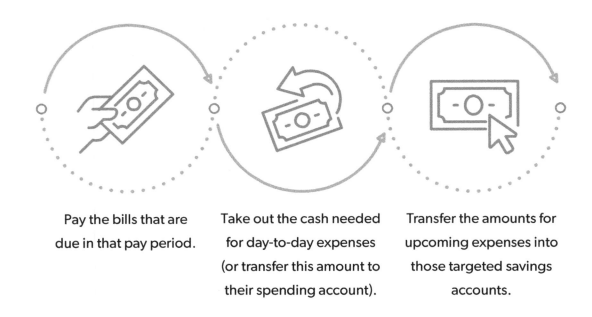

Pay the bills that are due in that pay period.

Take out the cash needed for day-to-day expenses (or transfer this amount to their spending account).

Transfer the amounts for upcoming expenses into those targeted savings accounts.

There's a little wiggle room in the system. For instance, if the big expenses (mortgage, car payments, etc.) happen in the first half of the month, pay those with the first paycheck of the month – and make the transfers into the savings accounts with the mid-month paycheck. Some clients like to fund savings accounts each pay period; others prefer once a month.

Setting up the new budgeting system requires some technical and online skills, a point that can be used to your advantage as a financial coach. Some people may have the drive and technical knowledge to do this on their own. Those might be the folks who leave their Discovery Session and "take it from there."

For others, however, it can be a challenge to set up online savings accounts, or perhaps they've never used Excel before. They need your help! It might take some courage for them to ask for it, so it's up to you to prompt that discussion. Some people also need their coach to ensure that they'll be accountable for doing the follow-through after the set-up work is completed.

With the extra money that a client has at the end of the month, we ask that they be intentional about how it is used. As mentioned earlier on the topic of goal-setting, I suggest that they set one goal at a time and that they plan at least 3 to 6 months ahead.

> "Many folks think they aren't good at earning money, when what they don't know is how to use it."
>
> – FRANK A. CLARK, AMERICAN WRITER AND CARTOONIST

Strategies For Paying Off Debt

Debt is one of the most common reasons people will seek you out as a financial coach. Many of your clients will have heard of, and even used, some of the most often-touted strategies for paying off debt:

 Dave Ramsey's "Snowball" strategy is paying off debt with the lowest balance first, while making the minimum payment on the others; then the next-lowest, and so on. I recommend this method sometimes for a person who either doesn't seem to have much motivation to tackle their debt or who needs to see a quick win – it's always great to see the lowest-balance credit card debt finally go away.

 Suze Orman's "Avalanche" strategy categorizes debt by interest rate and focuses on paying off the highest-interest debt first. I recommend this for clients who have gotten themselves into high-interest debt, such as a payday loan or high-interest credit card or for those clients who are committed and don't require any additional motivation of a "quick win."

Other experts suggest organizing debt (not including rent or mortgage) from highest monthly payment to lowest monthly payment. Then, pay the minimum amount on everything except that highest-payment debt until it's paid off. This method works well for the person whose cash flow is tight, while their income and expenses are fairly even. By working to get rid of their highest payment, it eventually frees up money in their budget to use for other goals, such as allowing them to build up emergency savings.

 I also have developed my own debt-payoff strategy that varies from any of these. I call it the "Most Emotional Baggage" strategy. If there's a debt that makes the client feel angry every time they make a payment – for whatever reason – that could be the one to tackle first. It might be divorce related expenses, or a scary but necessary surgery that resulted in a large out-of-pocket bill. Give your client permission to make paying it off a priority, to get it out of their life.

I consider it my job to share all four strategies with the client and map out each option for them. Remember, making lessons visual is a key component of their learning. I like the client to know the pros and cons of each option so they can feel confident choosing the one that is right for them.

There's an exercise on page 201 for the *Debt Payoff Thermometer*. It's a handy little graphic that you can give a client to help them track their progress, payment by payment. You'll find that any such visual aid can help keep people motivated, especially for big debts that are daunting. DebtFreeCharts.com has some really creative and fun visuals too.

Student Loan Debt

The minefield that is student loan debt is complex and ever-changing. There are private and public loans, subsidized and unsubsidized loans, loans from parents, and even loans that parents take out for their kids to attend college. It would be impossible to cover them all in this format. My belief is that the student loan crisis plays a major role in how people feel about their money and can significantly impede their drive to pursue passions, buy a home, or invest in other assets.

For financial coaching purposes, we tackle them the same way as any other debt or financial challenge. We help the client decide what they want to do about it and make a

Debt Payoff Thermometer

.... **GOAL**

$ . . . .

$ . . . .

$ . . . .

$ . . . .

$ . . . .

$ . . . .

$ . . . .

$ . . . .

$ . . . .

$ . . . .

$ . . . .

$ . . . .

DEBT

$ . . . .

Tips for Reaching Your Goals

- Write your goal debt in the banner at the top (ie. credit card or student loan).

- Write your amount of debt in the bottom of the thermometer (i.e. $2,000).

- Write in dollar amounts in each different level of the thermometer (divide total debt by 12).

- Color in each thermometer level as you reach that total.

- Put this on your fridge or somewhere you can see it.

commitment to do it. This means asking questions, not only about the debt and payment amounts, but about how much stress this is causing the client.

....

... the student loan crisis plays a major role in how people feel about their money...

....

Some research might be required, which you can assign to the client to help them learn about their options. They might consider refinancing their student loans for a lower interest rate or finding a repayment program that bases their monthly payment on their income rather than the amount of the debt. Some of my favorite resources for student loans are StudentLoans.gov, NerdWallet.com, StudentLoanHero.com, and StudentLoanPlanner.com.

In some career fields, people can have at least a portion of their student loan debt forgiven by agreeing to work in an underserved area – say, a nurse practitioner or dental hygienist in a rural community – for a certain period of time. Teachers or other education professionals who work in low-income schools can look into Teacher Student Loan Forgiveness. There is also a Public Service Loan Forgiveness program for people with federal student loans who work in some government public service or nonprofit agencies.

In short, it's the role of the financial coach to encourage the client to be aware of their choices, provide resources, and help them to sift through the complexities of student loans.

The Emergency Budget

The Emergency Budget is an exercise I do with clients and is a great example of taking a concept widely discussed (emergency savings) and taking it one step further. After a client has become comfortable with their budget, I'll copy and paste that exact budget into a separate Emergency Budget tab, and we start thinking about contingency plans in case of an emergency. We ask, *"Should an emergency happen tomorrow, what changes would we make to how we spend money?"* I observed early that most clients, when faced with an emergency, go into "emergency mode" - they naturally cut back and reduce spending. The purpose of the Emergency Budget is to be more intentional.

> ... if an emergency were to happen tomorrow, what changes would we make?

This really hit home in my own life when, some years ago, my husband Michael was working at a job that he truly disliked. He's such a happy-go-lucky guy that it would have to be very bad for him to dislike it that much! So, we talked it over and made the decision that he would resign.

The resulting questions – *"What will change for us financially when YOU leave your job? What cuts will WE have to make because YOU want to quit? How will this impact our lifestyle, and for how long?"* – we were making an already emotional decision even more super-charged and difficult.

If we'd had an emergency budget in place – not just emergency savings, but an actual plan in place that we could shift to – it would have been far less stressful, even when we were both in agreement that his leaving the job was the right thing to do.

What's in an emergency budget? To make one, we go through the clients' typical budget line by line to decide which personal expenses they would cut and which they would keep. What types of adjustments are they willing to make to live on less money? There is some guesswork, of course – if one person's job provides the couple's health insurance, the needs will be different if that person gets laid off.

We estimate dollar amounts a little bit high, just to be safe, and whatever the monthly emergency budget total turns out to be is our target amount for a 3-month or 6-month emergency savings account.

Too often, fate blindsides a person or a couple and the first thought is, *"What now?"* An emergency budget helps answer that question in a positive, proactive way. I hope you never need it – but it's better to have a plan to execute if you do. It's also smart to reevaluate the emergency budget annually, or during any major life change.

Determining Savings Rate

Teaching the concept of a savings rate and making this concept relevant to the client is another exercise I really enjoy. A client's savings rate is the amount of money, expressed as a percentage or ratio, which they deduct from their disposable income to set aside as a "nest egg" or for retirement. I explain to them that it's an important tool to help gauge their progress toward meeting their financial goals.

Some clients love calculating their savings rate and do it monthly; others are content to do it once or twice a year.

I use an exercise that I created, called *"Know and Grow Your Savings Rate."*

In this exercise, there are categories for:

Gross Income (income from all sources)

− *Taxes Paid*

_____

Net Income

For businesses, the categories are:

Business Revenue

− *True Business Expenses*

+ *Other Income Sources*
(rental property, gifts, Social Security, etc.)

_____

= *Net Revenue*

The "net" amount is basically the money that is leftover; the client gets to decide what to do with this amount. They won't necessarily be putting that money into savings or a retirement account. They might be using it to pay off credit card or consumer debt or making additional principal payments on a mortgage. The important thing is that they are using these funds to make some financial progress.

The spreadsheet automatically calculates the percentages of income going to these various priorities – and of course, the overall savings rate.

For the financial coach, the next step is to get the client to talk about how they feel about this number. Get them to reflect on it and think more deeply about it. If they're proud of it, that's terrific and you want them to acknowledge that! But you're also going to prompt them to take the next step.

"What dollar amount would represent a 1 percent increase?" I ask. (Take their net income and multiply it by .01 to see the actual amount they'd need to boost their savings rate by 1 percent.)

When we have that figure, ask, *"Are there some areas of your budget where we could cut back, challenge, adjust, eliminate, or negotiate to 'find' that amount?"*

As we've discussed before, the idea is to get clients to commit to doing a little more, so they can continue to build on the progress they've made.

Finding Side Hustles

In many cases as a financial coach, you will focus heavily on the client cutting their expenses and learning to live within their value system. But sometimes, what they need is more income. Some clients have never seriously considered what else they might do to bring in additional cash. I see one of my roles as opening their eyes to these possibilities.

According to a 2018 study from Jobvite, a recruiting and job-applicant tracking company, 31 percent of American workers have some type of side gig to make extra money. And the additional side-hustle income totaled an average of $686 a month, based on a survey of more than 1,000 workers by the personal finance website Bankrate.

In my experience, there are four things that often stop people from starting their own business, even just part-time:

1. They believe the old adage, *"It takes money to make money."* This is false! I began my financial coaching business from my dining room table, while working at another full-time job. For years, I can honestly say I had no expenses – no office, no business cards, or dedicated phone line. I didn't even have a name for it. I built my clientele by word of mouth, as I worked with people who got their financial lives on track and then told others about me. Remember, conversations create cash!

2. They don't have confidence that their business idea will work.

3. They fear that their idea or hobby won't work as a business.

4. They don't know what to do, on a day-to-day basis, to get started and keep up the momentum.

I tell clients, *"If there's something you enjoy doing or making, and you could get paid to do it, that would be the ideal situation, so do your research!"* The best way to counter a lack of confidence (#2) and/or fear (#3), as well as the "what to do next" dilemmas (#4), is with information. If you find that the barriers to entry are minimal, there's no risk, and not much money required out-of-pocket, then it really boils down to your own determination to take a leap of faith.

Yes, that's a really big deal! But if it results in extra money, extra energy, and a more fulfilled life, why not step outside your comfort zone?

If their side hustle or new gig is going to work for them, you'll want it to be something they are truly interested in or passionate about. On the next page you'll see a *Find Your Idea Grid*, which I developed to help people examine four categories of side businesses and choose one that both excites them and isn't too difficult to get started.

Once you have finished, if you find something in box B, you may have found the perfect business idea!

Find Your Idea Grid

REALLY EXCITES ME

A

B

DOESN'T EXCITE ME

C

D

TRICKY TO GET STARTED & MAKE $

EASY TO GET STARTED

Other Alternatives To Discuss

What can I get for free?

Finding connections, doing research, and having conversations might set you back the cost of lunch or coffee, but are basically free. There are places to design your own website free of charge. Touting your services on social media is free!

What can I borrow?

Does a neighbor have a high-quality printer you might use for your flyers? If your home isn't set up for client meetings, does a fellow entrepreneur have a quiet spare office or conference room you could use?

What can I trade or barter?

Can you offer a month of financial coaching to someone who has design, writing, or social media skills? A photographer who'll take a nice set of business headshots for you? Someone who's well-versed in eBay sales who could help you with the next item?

What can I sell?

Many cities have consignment shops for electronics, furniture, clothing, and more. Ask about their rules and plan to pick up some extra cash. Online sales offer a whole range of options, although they do take time to post and manage.

I often recommend that clients look at the website Side Hustle Nation or listen to the podcast, The Side Hustle Show. This site lists dozens of potential side businesses, from becoming a notary to keeping parking lots clean, designing t-shirts, managing vacation rentals, or baking (many states have so-called "home baking" laws that allow people to produce baked goods without a commercial kitchen by meeting some basic health and safety standards). There seem to be plenty of options for anyone with the drive to make some extra money – depending, of course, on what they'll need to spend to get started.

We can budget for that, too!

"Every accomplishment starts
with the decision to try."

– JOHN F. KENNEDY, PRESIDENT

Making A Legacy Drawer

I always ask clients if they have a will, trust, or estate plan, and whether it is current. I am surprised at how many either do not have these documents, haven't looked at them in years, or never considered whether or not they should have them.

Thinking about end-of-life plans isn't fun. Sometimes people have other, more urgent priorities when they come into coaching. Estate planning can also be expensive; not everyone has the funds to hire an attorney to do it. My role as a coach is not to tell them what type of estate documents are needed but to outline the steps they can take right away to make progress, such as begin saving for this expense and sitting down with an attorney.

In the meantime, I use the concept of a *Legacy Drawer* as a single, convenient spot to organize many of the key documents loved ones would need, and present it as a way to minimize their stress in the event of the client's death.

On the next page, you'll find a list of items to keep in your Legacy Drawer. The Legacy Drawer contents can be stored in a fireproof safe or anywhere it might be easy to access if needed, but also stay protected and safe.

Gathering the information for the Legacy Drawer always seems to be the task that clients put off the most. The process takes time to compile, and even the topic can be tough to broach with clients. However, they always feel better when they do it. So, you might break it up into smaller increments: *"Can you get one of these pages done by our next session? Can you get just one section finished?"*

Legacy Drawer

List of debts (amounts you owe)

List of monthly expenses (accounts, due dates, etc.)

Copies of will or trust and any Power of Attorney documents

Funeral instructions • Personal letter(s)

Contact information for important people
(family members, financial advisors, attorneys, insurance agents)

Financial information
(bank and investment account numbers, logins and passwords,
life insurance policies, drafts of personal budget)

List of assets - Things you own
(detail anything of particular value and what it might be worth)

Safe deposit box location and access information

Monitoring Credit Reports And Scores

I don't spend much time on this topic with my clients, but I encourage you to prioritize it if you feel differently.

I tell people about AnnualCreditReport.com, a site where folks can go to check their own credit reports annually, free of charge. I suggest they make a note on their calendar to pull one report from one company (Equifax, Experian, and Transunion) every four months – that way, it's a periodic check instead of a big, once-a-year look, without having to pay anything.

I like CreditKarma as a way for people to monitor their own credit scores. I don't think it is especially accurate, but it's a good ballpark for those who need to keep an eye on it.

One topic we discuss is how and why to freeze a credit report – not just the client's, but if their children have credit reports, or if they are caring for older family members. Both of these groups are susceptible to identity theft.

If a client receives a credit report and needs to dispute some items, we will discuss the dispute process and/or whether they need to bring in a third party to contact the credit bureaus on their behalf.

Goals And Skills To Shoot For

With all the exercises and skills you and your clients will be discussing, I found it helpful to determine ideal milestones for progress. As discussed earlier, every client goes at their own pace so it's important to keep in mind that this is simply the ideal scenario. Where would you like the client to be after a particular length of time? How should they be feeling and how may they be thinking differently? What new skills have they acquired during that time?

Here's where I see the ideal client at the end of our first month together:

✓ We've discussed their goals and they have a clear picture of their financial situation.

✓ They understand the specific behavioral changes it will take for them to make progress.

☑ We've set up their budget using the Ultimate Financial Power Plan, and they understand:

- What goes on it and what does not.

- Timing of bills, cash withdrawals, and savings transfers based on their paychecks.

- When (and for what) to use cash, debit, and credit cards.

- How to update the budget if needed.

☑ They've created their targeted savings accounts and set up their online bill-paying system.

☑ They're able to plan ahead for one to three months. The idea here is to get them comfortable with extending the budget on the spreadsheet from month to month so they can update it in a timely manner.

After three months of coaching:

☑ With their budgeting skills honed in, the client is able to update the budget, refine it based on planning worksheets, and consider the results before they make a big financial decision.

☑ The client is able to challenge their past budget assumptions and better align their spending to their values.

☑ We're able to turn our attention more to the future, to focus on a one-year vision rather than their immediate financial state.

☑ Couples have clearly defined tasks and open communication about their finances. They're working creatively through any of their financial differences.

☑ They can do three-month and annual planning exercises, and their monthly calendar of random expenses is completed.

- ✓ They have goals – one-month, three-month, six-month, and one-year – that include targets, a timeframe, and a milestone-and-reward system.

- ✓ They're able to recognize temptations and avoid or ignore those triggers.

- ✓ They're working on overcoming specific challenges based on their money mindset. If they have a bad month, they know how to get back on track and not let it throw them.

- ✓ They are able to turn some attention to creating an emergency budget if they haven't been able to do so earlier.

- ✓ Best of all, they feel a sense of accomplishment and excitement as their plans extend into the future. They're more intentional and more in control.

The ultimate goal, of course, is to replace their uncertainty, fear, and stress about money with confidence and clarity. Time and time again, I've seen that this is possible.

Chapter 07

Action Summary

☐ 1. Create tracking or planning worksheets for your clients on the of expenses you deem necessary (i.e. Medical, Gifts, Travel, Subscriptions, etc).

☐ 2. Think through your philosophy regarding the scenarios used in this chapter: debt payoff, student loans, visual trackers, emergency budget and savings, savings rate, side hustles, legacy drawer, and credit scores.

☐ 3. Make a list of other financial concepts you might come across and begin to think through how you might help the client to better understand those concepts. Seek guidance and insights from other financial coaches or resources so you can feel more prepared.

☐ 4. Develop new exercises for your clients based on some of the financial concepts, money, and budgeting ideas outlined in this chapter. Remember that as you continue to grow and learn, you will be able to craft new exercises easily!

IF YOU COULD PLAN FOR **75%** OF WHAT'S GOING TO HAPPEN TO **you financially,** WOULDN'T THE OTHER **25%** **BE SO MUCH EASIER** TO HANDLE?

• KELSA DICKEY •

I loved learning that I could try one way for a while and morph it into another thing. I now understand there are different seasons in your life and one approach might not work now but could work later on. Changing from 1:1 coaching to group coaching has made me more fulfilled and happy. It also helps my clients feel like they are a part of a community of like-minded people who are trying to achieve their financial goals.

HOLLY HOLBROOK

GRACE INSPIRED LIVING

Chapter 08

Branching Out:
Ideas For Growing Your Business

After you've been a financial coach for a while, you'll see the need to find ways to use your time more effectively, as well as the wisdom in branching into other areas of personal finance in order to grow your business. Developing some "value-added services" can help you do both.

How Do You Know When And How To Grow Your Business?

Your goal should never be to put your business on autopilot, always doing what you've always done. My weekly check-in – which I happen to sit down and do on Sunday afternoons – is a way for me to consider, *"What will fill my cup this week?"* Sometimes, I want to think about work as little as possible – say, if I've just finished a big project and want to take it easy. Other times, I've got an idea I've been mulling over that I'm excited about and want to tackle right away. From one week to the next, it might be completely different.

I also turn some of the same questions I ask clients on myself, to home-in on how things are going with the business: What's going well? What am I enjoying? What didn't go well? What do I find myself simply tolerating? I might also look to my own business or life coach for guidance.

In this chapter, I'll cover a few of the value-added services we've seen a need for at Fiscal Fitness Phoenix, and explain how we've found ways to address them and boost our business in the process.

Daily Money Management

This service happened purely by accident. After coaching one particular client – a very busy small business owner, who did a great job of learning the whole system of budgeting – he then said, *"All right! I understand the value of this and know how to do it myself – but I don't really want to. Can I just pay you to do it for me?"*

And I said, *"Sure. I could do that."*

I started managing his bill payments, transferring funds into spending and savings accounts, updating his budget, and so on. I imagined only ever doing this for clients, of course. I mean, why would anyone give me access to their bank accounts, Social Security number, usernames and passwords, if I hadn't been working with them?

And yet, when we added Daily Money Management (DMM) as a service on the Fiscal Fitness Phoenix website, I was astonished at how many people arranged to meet with me and were absolutely willing to hand over the reins to their financial lives.

In some cases, busy professionals need someone to take on the money management role for an elderly parent. But the people I worked with were, in most cases, small business owners who decided their time was better spent on growing their business and managing their business finances. Where I stepped in to help was in the area of their personal finances.

About 90 percent of DMM is paying someone's bills – but I'm vigilant about it, and I often find errors or discrepancies on those bills and look into them. In addition, I will look at clients' Credit Karma scores or check their credit reports for them. I will shop their insurance rates for them every year and check their declaration pages, just to make sure they're getting the best possible coverage for their money. And I keep in regular, weekly email contact to let them know what I'm doing and how we're progressing on their goals.

For coaches who would like to consider offering this type of service, here's how my process works:

The DMM Process

CONSULTATION

This truly is a consultation. The goal is to tell the prospective DMM client about the service, not to provide advice or guidance. We charge a small fee for a 30-minute consultation, which is then refunded if they show up for their session. Offering this refund helps minimize the "no-show factor."

EMAIL PACKET

After the consultation, the prospective client is sent an email that includes references, a copy of the contract, and a list of information I'll need from them, along with a date and time that we'll be following up.

MY REVIEW & ANALYSIS

This part of the process is similar to a Discovery Session – only I'm doing the work that the client would usually do and present to me. So, the more organized this client is up front, the lower their first month's bill will be. The client provides me access to all bank accounts, debit card numbers, bills, etc., and lets me know how each bill is usually paid. I spend time logging in, writing down notes and questions. I review 3 to 4 months of their banking activity, 3 to 4 months of bills and statements, and devise the plan.

STRATEGY SESSION

We meet for one hour (the first of two hour-long sessions per year). I walk them through the plan I have made for them. We talk about what they have coming up that we need to get ahead of – and then from there, I take over the bill-paying and budgeting responsibilities. I do not "take over" until this strategy session is complete and all questions are resolved.

DAILY MONEY MANAGEMENT BEGINS

When I am handling their personal finances, I'm billing by the hour, so I document my time by the minute. (Using Google sheets automatically tracks the time, so they can always see it.) The client has access at all times to their budget, so they can see what I've paid, what I'm about to pay, what's cleared their account, confirmation numbers, and so on. They set up separate bank accounts for bill-paying and their own daily spending (gas, groceries, etc.). I only use the bill-paying account; I don't look at their daily spending account.

WEEKLY REVIEWS

I send a weekly email, the subject line of which is either, 'Weekly Review: Action Required' or 'Weekly Review: No Action Required.' I want them to see that, week to week, I am keeping up with their finances. I might say, *"Here are some things I want you to be aware of, but overall, everything is going as planned."* Or I'll summarize what I put into savings, what got paid, and so on. When action is required, it might be letting them know that a bill came in higher than anticipated, or alerting them to a charge that they might not be aware of.

WEEKLY REVIEWS (CONTINUED)

Do I need to dispute this charge? I want them to know I am on the case and doing my job! Right in our contract for DMM clients, we state that, 'Any bill with an increase of more than 25% of the prior month's bill will warrant attention.' But we also state that 'investigation into the cause of the increase' will be the client's responsibility unless they authorize me to research it.

MONTHLY STATEMENTS

The client receives a monthly statement that reminds them to schedule their semi-annual session, but we do not hound them to do it. At Fiscal Fitness Phoenix, I've never had a client dispute their bill.

Remember, you are literally creating and maintaining a budget for this person or couple. You will need access to EVERYTHING – account numbers, usernames, passwords, and security-questions and answers. In some cases, even a power of attorney might be needed. So please consult with a business attorney on the best contract to use for DMM services with your client and/or take advantage of the American Association of Daily Money Managers organization (secure.aadmm.com).

Other DMM Considerations

In signing a contract for DMM services, we ask people for a minimum of three months. It's never been a problem – most have stuck with us for years.

I charge a flat monthly fee for this service, which includes up to two hours of administrative work per month, and the two one-hour strategy sessions per year. In the contract, however, we make people aware that the first month's bill will most likely be higher than expected because of the set-up time.

One perk we added is that after six months, I am responsible for any late fees or penalties – as long as there is proof that the bill or statement was provided to me (on paper or by email) with sufficient time to pay it.

When a decision is made to end DMM services, the contract also stipulates that a client give 30 days' written notice. This time is needed for us to update logins and passwords and remove me as a point of contact from their accounts. It also allows time for me to update them on their financial life and ensure a smooth hand-off.

At Fiscal Fitness Phoenix, we no longer offer Daily Money Management services. After years of providing this service, I checked in with myself just as I recommended you do and I realized that DMM work no longer filled my cup as much as the other projects we were launching. As my business continued to grow, something had to give and I decided to refer out all DMM work to other professionals. But it certainly adds value for some clients, and it is a perfect example of how you charge for the benefit to a person's life, rather than the time it takes. Some people are willing to pay for the peace of mind that their bills are being paid on time and their budget is getting some added scrutiny.

· ·

... you charge
for the benefit to
a person's life.

· ·

To learn more about managing people's money, I recommend checking out the American Association of Daily Money Managers. I also absolutely recommend getting liability insurance that covers errors and omissions, which includes such incidents as privacy violations or theft of personal information. Our liability insurance covers our employees as well, because I sometimes delegate to them.

Group Programs

If you have a handful of people who either come to you as an organized group or clients who are all at similar points in their financial journeys, you might consider creating a group coaching arrangement.

I've seen other financial professionals give group lessons or offer presentations to prospective clients, and those are great options if you want to do that. But I'm talking about creating a "next step" for clients with whom you are already working. My target client for what we call our Masterclass is the person who has already completed a 4-month or 7-month program. They've done the rigorous work, they've gotten the one-on-one coaching and attention, and they want to stay involved and learn more. They have excellent habits and skills in place, but they want continued reinforcement, support, and accountability that can be delivered in a group setting.

As a financial coach, there are major benefits for you from this approach. First, group sessions are a way to manage your time by sharing information with multiple clients that you'd otherwise have to share individually. This time-saver is necessary when you've built your business to the point that you have many loyal clients and want to stay connected with them, but find yourself covering the same points and concepts, over and over.

... build a community around your clients.

Second, it is also a wonderful way to build a community among your clients, getting them to feel comfortable with each other and serve as a support network for each other.

And third, putting these group sessions together challenges me to come up with new material and new strategies to recommend. It's a great motivator to constantly improve my repertoire of financial topics.

We charge a monthly fee per client for the 12-month Masterclass. The Masterclass is a hybrid that involves both group coaching and individual sessions. We've done it a couple different ways, and I'll explain both here so you can see it's a very flexible model.

For a long time, it consisted of a weekly group call and quarterly individual calls:

- Most of the group calls were Q & A sessions, but once a month, I would deliver fresh content: teach a new concept or skill, or challenge the group in some way. The call was recorded so that a group client, who couldn't be on the call but wanted to hear it, could access it and listen later.

- The 30-minute individual calls every quarter were designed around a 90-day goal, because we were meeting every 90 days.

More recently, the Masterclass has evolved into a different format:

- We have one group-coaching call a month, held online, in which I teach a specific concept and then open the call for questions. Instead of delivering this training live, as I do, you could record the lesson and send out the video for clients to watch at their leisure. I always enjoy the dialogue and discussion around what I am teaching, which is why live works best for me.

- Each group client also gets a 30-minute monthly call, which is handled by another coach in my office, to focus on individuals' 90-day goals. If you have a desire to hire other coaches or grow your team someday, this is a great option!

Masterclass members also are part of our Facebook group, which includes dialogue and talking points that dovetail with the topic I am covering on that month's group call. The Masterclass does not include private emailing or phone calls.

Interestingly, we've found people aren't at all shy about sharing their financial details in a group setting. Remember as you are developing your own group sessions that one of the main benefits for you is maximizing your time.

Accountability Programs

The final option we offer is the *Semi-Annual Session.* This is only for current or recent clients who are highly motivated and have been successful at managing their money. Clients are invited to choose this option if they continue to stay on track with their budgeting and financial goals on their own.

Semi-annual means two 60-minute sessions each year – one in June and one in December. The December session is the New Year Challenge, in which people set financial goals for the coming year. (For coaches, December works well for this type of program, because it typically isn't a busy month for new clients). In June, we see how well they're doing on those goals at the Mid-Year Check-Up.

You'll set your own rates, of course. We charge a set amount for the year, and clients pay on a recurring, monthly basis. For the client, it promotes self-reliance, personal responsibility, and financial focus, as they see the monthly amount that we bill in their budget. For the coach, it provides a steady source of monthly income.

Since these are only 60-minute sessions and there's six months of life happening in between, it is critical that people fill out a pre-session questionnaire. That's where you'll be able to pinpoint the issues you'll need to talk with them about during their session.

The Training Vault

Over the months and years of financial coaching, we've amassed an amazing number of resources. These include video tutorials about how to use various forms of technology (ex. Microsoft Excel), handouts, worksheets, and pep talks. Some third-party resources have also been provided to us to use with clients. We've put all of them in a single place online.

We call it the Training Vault.

 It is located on a members-only tab on our Fiscal Fitness Phoenix website. We created it as a safe landing spot to store information, in part so we wouldn't have to keep answering the same questions from clients. It is handy for them, but also a terrific time-saver for us.

When you design your website, make sure it has this capability – and that you'll be able to charge for access to your vault or "additional resources" area, which means it must be password protected or otherwise secured. Alternatively, you could use online course software through Thinkific or Teachable to create and manage your own content or Training Vault.

Corporate Wellness

Often a client will ask if you'd consider speaking to people in their company, and it's a good idea to do so. It might be a basic presentation or a "lunch and learn" session, and you could end up with some clients as a result.

But being part of a Corporate Wellness program is a different endeavor. You are getting paid to be there as a subject matter expert, so your goal is not to sell your services but to provide value to the company that has hired you for this role. Ideally, you want to build a relationship in which you're invited back, perhaps a couple of times a year.

I started in this field when I received a call from a local electric utility. They were transitioning to a new accounting system, meaning their 7,000 employees would be paid biweekly instead of on the 1st and 15th of the month. This, of course, would mean more paychecks – 26 instead of 24 – but smaller amounts per paycheck. The company was concerned about how the workers would respond to the change. They wanted a bid for my services to help their employees manage this transition.

I had no idea what to bid, so I sat down and thought about what I would need to know. If I had been one of these power company workers, how would I manage the changes in my pay structure, and how might I want to receive this information? My bid was in the five-figure range and on the day of my pitch, I remember feeling so nervous.

In hindsight, I bid too low! However, it was such a worthwhile experience. My company ended up getting the bid and prepared a workshop-style presentation, workbooks for the employees, and a three-video series. I was on-site at the company for about a month to host the workshops. During that time, I shifted my other clients to evening and weekend appointments to allow me to be at the utility company headquarters during the day.

It was exhausting but also rewarding. And it made us realize at Fiscal Fitness Phoenix that we could branch out into doing more Corporate Wellness. We hired a business-to-business coach who helped us with marketing expertise – since after all when most people think of "wellness," they don't think of financial wellness. So, financial coaches have a unique and much-needed role to play here.

To get this kind of business, it is necessary to connect with the decision-makers at a company. It might be the Human Resources director, or the CEO, or owner. Often, you can ask for referrals from clients.

> it's necessary to connect
> with the decision-makers...

The Corporate Wellness Process

Capabilities Briefing

The company execs will most likely want to know more about you, so this is the time to schedule a capabilities briefing. At this briefing you will summarize your qualifications, mention other companies you've helped, share your philosophy about money management, and so on. You will want to ask them plenty of questions about what they (or their workers) might need in terms of financial coaching. What types of employee benefits do they offer? What's the participation rate on their 401(k) program? Why might they want to bring you in?

Financial Stress Assessment

From there, we offer the company what we call a Financial Stress Assessment of the organization's employees. This involves surveying the workforce and offering a basic workshop on financial fitness, with a workbook for each employee.

Below is an example of some of the questions we ask in the Financial Stress Assessment:

- *On a scale of 1-10, what is your current level of financial stress?*

- *What is your hourly wage or annual salary?*

- *How confident are you about achieving your overall financial plan?*

- *What are your biggest causes of financial stress? Choose all that are applicable. (Provide a list from which they can choose).*

- *Have you ever taken care of your personal finances while at work?*

- *How many hours per week do you think you spend, on average, taking care of your personal finances while at work?*

- *How many days per month do you miss work completely?*

At Fiscal Fitness Phoenix, we've opted to only do this training for local companies rather than trying it remotely by video chat. Yes, it takes more time to do the surveys and workshops in person, but the personal engagement with the workers and managers is key. For the Financial Stress Assessment, we charge between $750 and $1,500, depending on the company size and number of people to be surveyed. We make it clear to the company that doing the assessment does not commit them to anything more than that, so it's an easy first step for them.

Perform the Survey

We used to send out the initial survey to the HR department and have them email it to workers to fill out and then we would compile the results. But we've seen employee participation skyrocket simply by talking with them in person instead. My theory is that people are nervous about filling something out on an employer's computer, even though they are promised anonymity because some of the questions are touchy – like, *"How many hours do you think you spend, on average, taking care of your personal finances while at work?" "Do you and your spouse fight about money?" "Do you miss workdays having to take care of, or as a result of stress from, your personal finances?" "How much money do you have in savings?"*

We have found that face-to-face, workers are surprisingly candid about their answers and grateful for the opportunity to talk about this topic.

Share the Results

We then compile the results and schedule a strategic debriefing to relay the overall information to the company – never individual workers' results, of course. There's a lot of research out there already about how much financial stress is costing companies in the U.S., but we've found most senior managers have convinced themselves that it doesn't apply to THEIR companies or THEIR workers! So often, the survey results are a real eye-opener.

We add up the hours people spend at work on their personal finances and multiply it by the average worker's pay, for a valid estimate of lost time and money. And at that point, we can logically pitch the idea of a Corporate Wellness program to get employees onto better personal financial paths, lower their stress levels, and make them more effective on the job. Combined, this will save the company more, in terms of productivity, than what they'll pay for our services.

Hold the Workshops

The program is typically a series of workshops – monthly, quarterly, perhaps twice a year – with spouses encouraged to attend. We can schedule them for lunchtimes, evenings, weekends, whatever works best. Sometimes it's a 90-minute session, other times 2 hours.

Topics include:

- Create Your Ultimate Financial Power Plan (how to budget)

- Goal Setting (how to get out of debt and save for targeted goals)

- Optimize Your Work Benefits (401(k) accounts, insurance options, etc.).
  We bring in one of our financial advisor referral partners for this workshop.

- We always design one workshop specifically based on input from the employees.
  What else do they want to know more about?

The company can pay a little bit more to make our toll-free hotline available, so we can answer workers' individual financial questions. We also offer an additional service of coming for a full day or two and holding individual breakout sessions with employees who sign up.

We give companies a few program options at different prices and, in most cases, allow them to pay by the month for 12 months.

Your competition in this area is the local banker who might come in to do a one-time talk about budgeting or credit – free of charge. So, it's important to point out how much more extensive and effective your program will be. And of course, with the Financial Stress Assessment results, you've got everything you need to make your case about its value.

The sales process can be challenging for a Corporate Wellness program. It might not fit into the company's budget that year, and you'll get a, *"Great idea! Come back in six months."* Or it might have to be cleared with several layers of company executives, which can take an interminable amount of time. It sometimes depends on how effectively the HR team can advocate for the employees to their higher-ups. It might help to offer to talk with the CEO yourself, rather than have an HR person serve as the go-between.

Our goal is never to be a one-day workshop provider. We want to build a relationship with the company and be of longer-term benefit to its people. This involves building trust, which requires more than a single encounter with them. Your ideal corporate client is the company where management understands this and wants to invest in its employees.

Determining Corporate Clients' Needs

The capabilities briefing for company executives is much like your Discovery Session with an individual client. Here are some questions that might be helpful to pose when you're meeting with them to pitch the idea of a Corporate Financial Wellness program:

- *Tell me why the company is interested in financial literacy/budgeting training for your employees.*

- *Did you see or hear something that led you to want this?*

- *Does your Human Resources department ever get requests for help with workers' financial issues?*

- *How would you describe employees' mood or the overall atmosphere around money?*

- *Have you tossed around any thoughts or ideas in the past about a financial wellness program or what you'd like to see in it?*

- *Does the current level of employee financial health visibly impact profitability, customer service, productivity, or any other area of the business?*

- *What impact do you hope to see by offering this training to your employees?*

- *Is there a preferred timeline for implementing this?*

- *We customize our training based on the benefits you offer, so what types of benefits do workers receive? (401(k)? Matching? Health/Vision/Dental? Deductibles and copays? Employee Assistance Programs? Wellness activities?)*

- *Given all the other things on your plate, where is this issue on the priority list? Are there resources in place to address it?*

- *Are there upcoming activities, initiatives, dates, or deadlines on your calendar that we'd need to be aware of or work around?*

- *What is your budget for this initiative?*

Being Intentional With Your Business

If financial coaching is the right path for you, you'll soon be well on your way to starting and growing your business. It's fun, exciting, challenging, and scary, all at the same time. So, I want to remind you at this point to schedule regular check-ins with yourself. You'll find a Life Reflection and Goal Planner on page 232, which you'll find useful for yourself as well as your clients yearly or semi-annually.

At the beginning of this chapter, I mentioned never putting my coaching business on autopilot. So at least once a year, I recommend reflecting on the year.

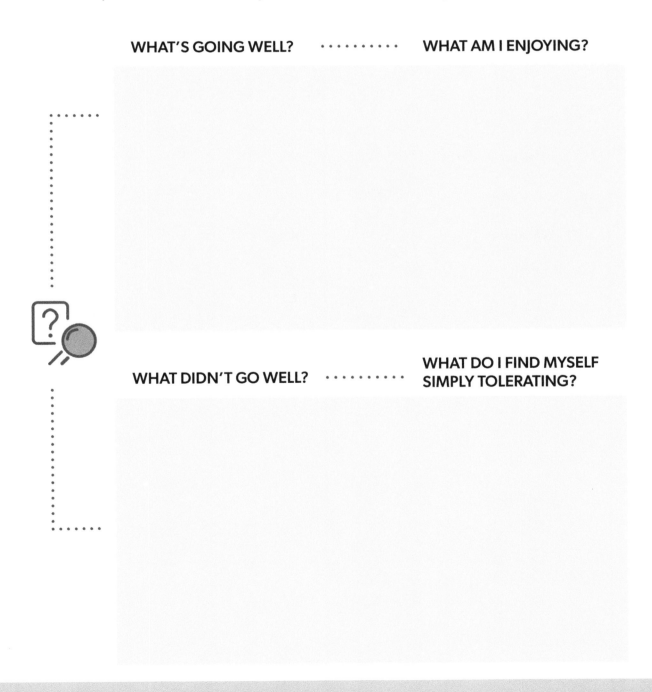

WHAT'S GOING WELL? · · · · · · · · · · **WHAT AM I ENJOYING?**

WHAT DIDN'T GO WELL? · · · · · · · · · **WHAT DO I FIND MYSELF SIMPLY TOLERATING?**

Life Reflection Goal Planner

WEEK OF:

UPCOMING EXPENSES/NEEDS/WANTS:

AREA OF LIFE	SATISFACTION 0-10	GOAL OR INTENTION
FAMILY		
FRIENDS		
HEALTH: MENTAL		
HEALTH: PHYSICAL		
HEALTH: EMOTIONAL		
PROFESSIONAL		
SOCIAL • FUN • PLAY		
SPIRITUAL		
FINANCIAL: PERSONAL		
FINANCIAL: BUSINESS		
FINANCIAL: SHORT TERM		
FINANCIAL: LONG TERM		
HOME/ENVIRONMENT		
SERVICE TO OTHERS		

ACTIONS OR CHANGES:

Looking ahead should be a positive experience if you have a goal or plan, something potentially fun and interesting to look forward to.

Remember the four key questions to ask yourself:

What are all the ideas I have for my business? (Yes, list them!)

Which of these ideas excites or intrigues me the most? Prioritize them.

What problems from the current year need solving or fixing?

Brainstorm solutions for them.

To ensure action, block off time on your calendar to put the top-priority ideas into motion. Don't forget, however, to also schedule family time, travel time, days off, and so on. These priorities are a necessary part of bringing balance to the sometimes hectic process of starting or expanding your coaching business. When we sit down to do our annual reflection and planning, we block off time for family and vacations first.

This approach of intentional reflection can adapt easily to other aspects of your life: health and fitness goals, home improvements, travel plans.

I also believe it is important for coaches to have coaches. It might be a business coach or a life coach, but I can cite at least three good reasons to consult with a professional guide who can provide a wise, objective point of view about your issues and concerns:

We're often "in our own head" too much.

We're thinking about something and trying to coach ourselves about it before the thought is even fully formed. We don't allow ourselves to simply feel whatever we're feeling, without shoving it through the "coaching filter."

It can show others that we believe in the power of coaching.

It's much easier to share with a client how powerful coaching can be – how it can transform lives, and give people clarity and excitement – when you have experienced it yourself. You might come away with some pointers for making your own coaching style more effective, as well.

Talking it out can be invaluable.

It's helpful to be on the receiving end of advice. It's also good to be reminded about what it feels like to be vulnerable – to share something you might be embarrassed about, or don't have answers for. Your clients feel that way on a regular basis! So, knowing how it feels to BE coached can benefit you in multiple ways.

> "To be successful, you have to have your heart in your business, and your business in your heart."
>
> – THOMAS WATSON SR., FORMER CEO OF IBM

> **Your business will only grow by the amount you are willing to grow yourself.**

Business goals and focus are important, but it's important to ask yourself, "How can my business serve me? How does it complement or add to my life in other areas?" One mistake I see new business owners make – and I'm certainly guilty of this too – is not looking at their business from a holistic approach. If you only create goals and ambitions for your business, and you suffer a bad month or are in a rut, it could lead you to feel discouraged about your life in general.

Your business is just one part of your life and it will have ebbs and flows. Work diligently to prevent the situation in which your happiness hinges almost solely on the success or status of your business.

Your business will only grow by the amount you are willing to grow yourself. And just as I tell our clients: change is hard. I want to remind you about the reasons you decided to take the leap into becoming a financial coach. At the very start of this book, I asked you to define your 'Why.' The tough days, the challenging conversations, the mistakes we feel embarrassed about – that's when it's important to remember your why and feel it deeply.

As financial coaches, we have the ability to completely transform a person's life for the better. All of us together can create a huge shift in our world – where folks feel less stressed, more hopeful, more fulfilled, and more creative in their life's pursuits – all because of the coaching we provide. We can overcome any obstacle or setback with that in mind.

"There is no power for change greater than a community discovering what it cares about."

- MARGARET J. WHEATLEY, AUTHOR

Chapter 08

Action Summary

☐ 1. Identify any "Next Level" programming you may want to add: Daily Money Management, Group Programming, and/or Corporate Wellness offerings.

☐ 2. Plan ahead and set goals in your business.